Become Who You Are

WHY DEPRESSION IS A SIGN OF GROWTH

by
Troy Ewing Psy.D.

Copyright © 2013 Troy Ewing Psy.D.
All rights reserved.

ISBN: 0615729517
ISBN-13: 9780615729510

Contents:

Chapter 1. 4
Misalignment of Your True Identity

Chapter 2. 12
False Identities

Chapter 3. 24
How Depression is a Sign of Growth

Chapter 4. 38
Discovering Your Inner Struggle

Chapter 5. 58
Why Your Brain Can Be Your Worst Enemy Or Your Best Ally

Chapter 6. 76
Breaking The Pattern of Bad Relationships

Chapter 7. 100
Beginning Phases for Change & Growth

Chapter 8. 118
Maintaining Motivation For Change

Chapter 9. 132
Improving And Maintaining Your Mood

Chapter 10. 150
Putting It All Into Daily Practice

Chapter One

Misalignment of Your True Identity

*"If you do not change the direction,
you may end up where you are heading."*

-Lao Tzu-

If you have ever experienced negative emotional states such as depression and anxiety, then you will think it a bit unusual when I say to you, "Depression is a good thing." I know. I know. It sounds hard to believe, and I am sure no other psychologist has ever smiled at you and said, "I am glad you are depressed." But I will say it to you now because, although depression itself is most unpleasant, depression can actually be a sign of growth or at least a precursor to potential for growth.

Depression is an uncomfortable emotional state, one we ultimately want to change. However, just as there is some discomfort and pain when physical growth occurs, there will be some emotional distress when psychological growth occurs as well. Much of the time, the primary symptom we experience when psychological growth has occurred is depression. To understand how depression is indicative of psychological growth, we have to look at our psychological development.

Psychological development begins at birth and progresses throughout our lives as we learn and interact with the world. Early on, our psychological growth is largely dependent on our family interactions. We learn language, speech, cultural nuances, behaviors, and even our views of our self and self worth through our family interactions. We learn how to view ourselves and we learn the behaviors we should engage in to interact appropriately with our family. Humans have an innate identity that develops over time that includes our natural predispositions, talents, and desire for self-expression.

When we are young, we are more dependent on others to help aide our identity development and understand our place in society and the world. If our early learning coincides with our natural predispositions and our family system is balanced in a healthy way, we develop a strong sense of self and self-efficacy. We tend to be happy and productive individuals. However, if early learning consists of unhealthy expectations or there is an imbalance in our family system, then it shifts our identity development and impacts who we are and our behaviors.

When there is an imbalance in a family, we develop two identities without being aware of it. We have a **false self** (a learned identity) and a **true self** (an innate identity). When the true self overshadows the false self, there is minimal depression and we develop with relatively healthy behaviors and emotions. However, if the family system is imbalanced to a significant degree, then a strong false self develops and we live an unfulfilled life. The puzzling piece here is that if a false self is put into place initially, and then the true self begins to develop later, we start to experience depression and often can develop self-destructive behaviors.

Why depression occurs if you later start to develop a stronger true self is the result of an identity struggle between whom you were *taught* to be and who you *really are*. Each identity fights for self-expression. We are rarely aware of this common struggle that challenges many of us, but it is there, quietly smoldering and impacting our moods and behaviors, without us being any wiser as to the cause of our depression or our self-destructive behaviors.

Two opposing identities can develop from imbalanced or unhealthy early learning experiences. Typically, depression is not the direct result of the false self being left unchecked. Depression occurs when the two opposing identities have come to a stalemate. When the false self is fully active and does not have the conflict with the true self, you might be apathetic and unfulfilled, but not in great distress. There is no force acting against the false self and no self-reflection. When both sides, the false self and the true self, find equal expression and neither side is able to outshine the other, you get lost in the conflict and emotionally begin to experience depression. You engage in destructive behaviors, negativistic thinking, or self-sabotaging behaviors without ever knowing why you are feeling the way you do or why you push those whom you care about away. You are caught in the struggle between the true self and the false self.

Depression is basically the middle ground, the stalemate. It means that you are not tethered to a false identity completely, nor are you free to express your true self completely. Depression means that something is impeding the false self and the true self equally to a point that it prevents happiness from being fully actualized. The potential for happiness and growth is there. All you need is a little push to the other side to live a self-fulfilled and content life. Depression is a sign of growth because it shows that your true self is there, holding back the false self that would otherwise lead you to an unfulfilled and inauthentic life.

To give you a better idea of the struggle, picture a river flowing steadily without being impeded. This unrestricted flow of water is representative of your identity in general—whether it is the true self or the false self. Now place a giant boulder in that river to oppose that flow. What happens? Turbulence, loud noise, and a disruption of the natural flow, right? Once something acts against the natural flow or holds the river back in some way, friction causes unsettled waters to emerge in the otherwise smooth flowing river.

If something holds back the natural development of your true self, or even your false self, the imposing obstacle causes friction and disruption in the development of the identity with the end-result of unpleasant emotions such as depression, irritability, and anger.

Your identities and emotions act in much the same way as a river. The true self has a natural progression if it is left unchecked by a false self. Conversely, the false self will develop and progress naturally through the experience of negative emotional states if they are left unchecked by the positive interactions of the true self.

If you are experiencing depression or unpleasant emotions, it means that a boulder has been placed in your path and it is somehow impeding the natural progression of your identity. To improve the resulting depression, all you have to do is to remove as much of the boulder that is the false self and let the unrestricted flow of your true self continue to lead you toward a peaceful, fulfilling life.

Like moving any giant boulder, removal of the false self is not that easy, especially if the false self was instilled at an early age. It takes time and practice to remove the entrenched false self and false identities. Just as a boulder is mired deep in the mud, the earlier we learn maladaptive thinking and behaviors, the more entrenched they are in our minds and the more difficult it is for us to unlearn them.

To give you an idea of what I mean, let me ask you how old you were when you first learned to ride a bike. When was the last time you rode one? Even if it has been years since you rode a bike, you can most likely jump on one and remember how to balance and peddle it enough to get you down the street without falling over.

Whether it is riding a bike, or interpersonal interactions, our behaviors, once repeated and mastered, are exceedingly difficult to forget. With each exposure to an environment and the repetition of a behavior, you start to modify your brain's physical structure and begin to "hardwire" this learning into your brain. The more you do something, the greater the neural connections throughout your brain, and the harder it is to extinguish these behaviors as we age and repeat these behaviors with conscious and subconscious repetition.

If you have ever wondered why you attract the same dysfunctional person in a relationship, or you keep making the same destructive mistakes at work or in your personal life, the hardwiring of learned behaviors allows you to continue to make these mistakes and repeat the damaging behaviors. Sometimes, no matter how many promises you make to change your patterns, after a while, you fall back into the unhealthy behaviors because this hardwiring cannot be unlearned without specific attention and strategies. We will discuss these strategies in later chapters.

Although we continue to learn and modify our behaviors and interpersonal relationships throughout our lives, our early experiences are the most crucial because our mind is quite literally shaping itself and molding itself by our experiences. Our minds are a blank slate, relatively speaking, when we are born. From birth, you will basically have all the brain cells you will ever have (Myers 1993). However, there are thousands of neural connections developing in your brain throughout your lifetime, with the most exponential growth during your early childhood. These developing neural connections are responsible for your ability to walk, talk, learn language, and remember certain behaviors. These neural connections set your behavioral programs and allow you to learn social interactions and repeat behaviors that are contributory to survival and adaptive to the surrounding environments.

Our early family and social interactions often create the false self and false identities because we learn how to adapt to an unhealthy environment. Our brain makes us proficient in executing the behaviors. When you encounter a "normal" environment or a healthy situation, but you have a history of being proficient in how to navigate unhealthy environments, you will struggle and ultimately reveal the false self that impairs your progress in healthy environments.

The earlier you learn a false identity and the more you repeat the associated behaviors, the harder it is to rid yourself of them because they are becoming hardwired into your brain. The more hardwired they are, the more they will reveal themselves in every aspect of your life. You modify your life and behaviors to match the unhealthy environments in which you were most comfortable and are most proficient in navigating.

Let's take a look at false identities in more depth. You may recognize the most common ones. We will explore how they begin and how they can further impact your life and contribute to depressive symptoms and the unhealthy behaviors that sustain these symptoms.

Chapter Two

False Identities

"Until you make the unconscious conscious, it will direct your life and you will call it fate."

-Carl Jung

False identities can develop with exposure to a single traumatic event, such as a sexual assault, physical assault, or witnessing some horrific event. However, most false identities develop over time, with repeated exposure to unhealthy interpersonal interactions in the family relationship or social environment.

False identities are insidious and develop gradually as you are repeatedly exposed, and adapt to, unhealthy environments. When who you are or who you are meant to be (your true self) starts to be overshadowed by conflicting external information from an unhealthy environment or family interaction, an emotional unrest develops and grows into the adoption of a negative and skewed self-concept, called a *false identity*. The emotional unrest that emerges from having two opposing identities often finds its way into expression via unhealthy or destructive avenues unless it can be channeled into more healthy ones.

Let me give you an example to help clarify. Say there is a family of four—a father, mother, and two sons ages fifteen and four. Two years ago, the father lost his job and began to drink heavily. For all intents and purposes, the father is now an alcoholic. The mother has undergone stress over the past few years and is now experiencing an episode of serious depression. When the father comes home, he is upset, angry, and volatile. The mother is weeping, emotionally drained, and distant.

The fifteen-year-old is able to leave the family unit during the day to attend high school and interact with peers and his girlfriend during and after school. The four-year-old, however, remains at home the entire day with a depressed and emotionally drained mother. When the father gets home, he is volatile toward the young child and the mother. Any attempts by the four-year-old to derive affection from the angry father are futile and met with rejection and criticism.

The child is starting to learn his place in the world. He will begin to modify his behavior in order to feel connected to the family unit to try to rebalance the family dynamics that have been set off kilter by the dysfunctional parents. The four-year-old may become withdrawn and self-punitive to align with the emotionally detached family message being disseminated overtly and covertly by the father and mother. He may also try to combat the withdrawal by gaining attention through becoming overly involved in trying to appease the parents. He might even assume many of the parental responsibilities such as cooking and helping to take care of the other family members.

The four-year-old will observe the parental behaviors that seem to appease them and begin to mimic those behaviors. For example, the child may grab a beer from the refrigerator to hand to the father when he gets home. Or, he may hug the mother when she has episodes of crying, or otherwise be doting to her needs. In other words, the child has begun to anticipate the emotional needs of others and begins to change his behavior in an attempt to bring harmony to the household and feel connected to the distant parents. Thus, he has begun the adoption of a false identity.

Rather than having the child's personality develop independently, the family system has begun to shift his personality to fit in a dysfunctional environment. We will discuss how this family environment can cause the development of certain personalities and behavioral patterns in a moment, but, for now, we will explain a bit more about how the environment impacts our personality development.

When an unhealthy parent, family member, or a highly domineering figure in a family system shows negative emotions or reinforces maladaptive behaviors, the emotional intensity of the unhealthy parent and the family system's disquiet filters through the entire family unit. In the above example, the aggressive, alcoholic father affects the mother and both children. However, it is the youngest member that is affected to the greatest degree.

The children will be influenced more than the mother in this type of unhealthy environment because they lack previous learning of their own self-worth. Their self-worth and learning is dependent entirely on the family system. The youngest members are impacted to the greatest degree because they do not have other social systems they can step into to validate their positive and independent traits that foster the true self. The youngest members of the family have no safe retreat. They have nowhere to turn outside of the unhealthy family unit. The mother has access to coworkers, social agencies, family, and friends to help her filter out some of the negative effects of the inaccurate messages disseminated by the father. The younger the family member, the more dependent on the family system he is and the less social resources he is able to utilize.

How far each of the individual family member's self-view is skewed depends on the severity of the inaccurate message, the frequency with which the inaccurate message is delivered, and the access to other positive feedback. The longer the negative feedback is received, as mentioned in Chapter One, the greater the degree of hardwiring the person will have, making it more difficult to unlearn the unhealthy behaviors.

Although the same environment affects the entire family unit, causing false identities to develop in each member, exactly how each person learns to cope with the situation and future social interactions depends on many factors. If the child is naturally a social, extroverted child, he will begin to experience a sense of dissonance or a sense of emotional disconnect as his social predisposition is met with rejection and anger from those in his withdrawn family world. The child has to rebel angrily to gain negative attention, adopt a dominant role of caretaker to the family, or become an overachiever in social roles and games. Or, if the child attempts to garner affection from family members but is repeatedly frustrated, he or she may become sullen, passive-aggressive, and wait for family members, friends, or significant others to ask why he is down and depressed.

The child that experiences a less than perfect home-life will often get noticed by becoming the pseudo-parent and adopt the household responsibilities of cooking, cleaning, and attending to the emotional needs of the parents and other family members. No matter how the child goes about gaining emotional attachments and feedback from family and friends, he will live an inauthentic life. He will be modifying himself to counteract the imbalance of the family and filling the emotional void created within the unhealthy environment. He thereby has successfully adopted a false identity.

Whenever a family system or relationship forces a person to adapt to an unhealthy environment, over time, in order for the person to "survive" and feel less pressure from the system, that person has to adapt to the system or completely rebel against it. This process creates a false identity and persona for the person trying to adapt and survive the imbalanced environment.

The false identity is developed and sustained because when the person engages in learned behaviors, he receives less pressure from the environment and some reward for engaging in the behaviors. Even though the reward or positive feedback may be less than perfect, it is a reward nonetheless and a deviation from the overt negative messages. For example, when the four-year-old gets his father a beer, he may receive a halfhearted praise. When the child asks for a hug, he may get rejection or worse.

The adoption of a false identity is a way to initially feel connected to the family and receive some form of emotional connectivity to that environment. However, the greater the connection to the unhealthy environment and the stronger the false self, the greater the impairments in every social and interpersonal interaction you will have as you age and become an adult.

The internal frustration or emotional unrest from dealing with a false self that is damaging to your true self ultimately leads to external displays of unhealthy behaviors or significant emotional distress.

The stronger the misalignment between your true self and the false self, the greater the strength and fuel the false self will derive from the struggle and the more destructive overt behaviors will become. A growing misalignment between the true self and false self causes emotional distress or "pressure" that actively fuels the false self. It becomes more difficult to maintain the emotional pressure without it spilling out to affect social interactions and self-views. Unhealthy behaviors that were once confined to the unhealthy family system begin to splash over into social and personal interactions. The emotional energy becomes too great to control and leaks out into social engagement.

It is often others closest to us that are the first to see the unhealthy behaviors we may exhibit. They can recognize the emergence of the *false identities* and try to assist us in changing them or getting the help we need. However, when we are unaware of the struggle of our own false identity operating inside of us, we are resistant to help or change. It's not until we recognize the true self and better identify and tackle the false self that we can make lasting change.

How can you recognize the overt signs of false identities in yourself or others? Usually, the first cue of having a false identity will be behavioral in nature. These behavioral cues consist of actions, thoughts, or emotions that are self-destructive, self-effacing, passive-aggressive, or even violent. These behavioral cues can consist of any form of engagement in self-destructive behaviors like drinking excessively, promiscuity, fighting, and emotionally pushing people away when they begin to get close to you.

Behavioral cues are typically the easiest to observe because they are overt and ostensible displays of distinctive actions such as fighting, yelling, and social strife. However, sometimes the most invasive and damaging cues for what is fueling the behavioral displays are emotional and inward in nature. We often do not even notice these cues until they begin to alter the true self and our behaviors significantly. They tend to be more distressing emotional states and negative thinking that begin to damage our self-concept, self-worth, self-esteem, and mental wellbeing overall. There are also the emotional cues such as depression, anxiety, suicidal thinking, pessimistic thinking, social withdrawal, self-injurious behaviors, social avoidance, passive aggressive anger, etc. It is not until the false self is understood, recognized, and highlighted that change can begin. Recognition is the first step.

Although there are many false identities formed in an unhealthy family system, there are four primary examples that you may see in yourself or in others.

FALSE IDENTITY PERSONAS

Overt signs of false identities abound in our lives. You may be one of these or know a few friends that live life in fast-forward with a "**Super-Producer Persona.**" Super-producer personas seem to be caught in a perpetual cycle of accomplishment. They seek to accomplish any and all goals they possibly can in their personal and professional life. They seem as though there is never enough time in the day to accomplish all the goals they have set for themselves. They never finish a project without another lined up to replace the completed task.

These people prepare lunch for every family member, organize the life of their spouse or partner, and seem to seek out leadership roles in both their professional and personal life. They seem to accomplish everything and are so busy that there is little time for things including a thirty-second hug for their children before school because there is little time to waste.

This super-productive person is one option of adapting to a false identity, and most likely the more positive of the various options involving an emotionally detached family.

The "**Invisible Persona**" is a false identity that develops when the person is forced to adopt a helpless victim role to balance the unhealthy family unit. Typically, this personality develops when the environment involves an overly domineering parent, violent or volatile home-life, or a critical and demeaning parent. For this type of personality, physical, emotional, sexual, or psychological harm will result for them getting noticed or drawing attention from the family or its members. This personality operates in many people in varying levels of severity, depending on the seriousness of the threat and the length of the threat in the family system.

Invisible-personas continually find that they are walked on, overlooked, ignored, or overly abused by others on an ongoing basis. They become victims of bad relationships and seem to be the doormat for every selfish and arrogant person in their environment. They have simply learned to avoid conflict. Their early environment did not provide enough positive reinforcing feedback to allow them to feel self-worth. They gravitate toward abusive relationships, failure, and seem perennially trapped in disappointment. Friends quickly tire of dealing with the helplessness of hearing the same bad relationship story. Without realizing it, these friends begin to offer criticism and thereby serve to further reinforce the invisible-persona personality.

Some of the symptoms of this type of personality are eating disorders, depression, abuse, and drug and alcohol dependency. They gravitate toward emotionally negative expression such as "gothic" music, tattoos, piercing, or anything else that allows them to garner attention from self-defacing or negative and dark attention. The seemingly inexplicable gravitation toward things that are self-effacing is due to their internal distress seeking to be acknowledged. Their art, piercing, and poetry show a hint of anger directed toward the self, and is a way for the true self to advertise something is wrong. The person has been forced to adapt and the anger is the true self's attempt to rebel against the inaccurate self of the invisible person. Because the person does not know about the struggle, he/she is caught in a cycle of self-anger, dangerous and destructive behaviors and activities.

The anger expressed in the adoption of a false self is not always internal. At times, the anger is external and is a sign that another false identity persona has been adopted. With the "**Explosive Persona**," the person seems to be always bordering on a violent outburst. This persona typically affects men but can affect women as well. This type of person seems to radiate anger with every pore and fiber of his/her being. You may feel unable to communicate with the person lest they attack you verbally. Explosive personas are emotionally distant and seem to be preoccupied with something that has angered them all the time. Friends will avoid conflict with them due to the rage that seems to linger just beneath the surface. Although explosive personas seem to be leaders and often strive to attain positions of power, they ultimately engage in destructive behaviors that involve alcohol abuse or legal run-ins.

This type of personality develops almost entirely from a violent home where the patriarch exhibits similar traits. The person that grows up in this environment will have strife with men in life and often will engage in domestic violence. The child felt powerless, witnessing a volatile parent or violent environment. Rather than turn this anger inward, the person turns it outward in an attempt to dominate others. Any slight or perceived challenge, either physically or emotionally, and he/she resorts to anger as a defense mechanism in an effort to reclaim the power that was denied from an early age. The result is a life of fights, relationship difficulty, and legal trouble. The person goes through life creating the same sense of danger and uncertainty that he/she experienced as a child and pushes it onto others. This is one of the most destructive false identity personas because it impacts others to the greatest degree and further creates the cycle of anger and victimization in others.

The **"Friction Persona"** is a newer and increasingly popular persona, validated and personified in modern media, especially in reality television. This friction-persona strives for conflict and thrives in being the center of attention through Machiavellian means. Individuals with this persona may be overtly or covertly abrasive and hyper-critical of everyone and everything, bringing friction and social chaos to every social or personal relationship. They start rumors or plant seeds for strife by being two-faced or conniving. They strive to be in social interaction constantly and have attention focused on them. In modern media, reality shows depict housewives arguing, people surviving on a deserted island by getting "one up" on the other, or musicians fighting with one another. The friction brings attention, thereby reinforcing these behaviors financially and emotionally. This persona begins early on typically in a neglectful household where the child only gets attention through acting up or getting into trouble. Those with friction persona seem to be both almost sociopathic in their need for destruction, while simultaneously craving any form of attention coupled with a desire for constant social interaction. This is a more emerging and modern false identity, and will be growing rapidly with the vast exposure and reinforcement it is receiving from the public and the media.

Although these four types of false identity personas are rather common, not everyone exposed to an unhealthy family environment will develop an unhealthy personality or false identity. Some are able to emerge relatively unscathed. However, some are impacted more than others depending on the extent of the dysfunction of the social or family environment. We all have some struggle waging within us from our previous learning. However, even though we face struggles that stem from our early environment, the results or signs of that struggle are not necessarily a bad thing. In fact, without some form of an emotional struggle, you would never grow, love, or pursue happiness.

Chapter Three

How Depression is a Sign of Growth

"Without a struggle there can be no progress."

-Frederick Douglas-

As with physical growth, emotional growth is preceded by a little pain. In the psychological sense, pain comes in the form of anxiety, depression, and anger. In some instances, this pain of depression and anxiety does not arise until later in life when things appear to be getting better.

The majority of depressive episodes and anxiety symptoms can first arise when the false identity and true self are beginning to face off and they reach a stalemate for the first time. This typically does not happen when you are amidst the chaos of a dysfunctional family or life situation. The struggle does not occur until you begin to receive reinforcing feedback from another source that strengthens the true self and weakens the false self. Depression that comes after you accomplish a goal, after a mid-life crisis, or when everything seems to be going well in your life, are all signs of the reawakening of your true self.

Although the onset of depression can be viewed as a good indication that change is imminent and your true potential is available and free for expression, depression is not something you want to continue indefinitely. It has potential to cause physical damage. Sustained depression, if left unchanged, has been shown to be associated with damage to the hippocampus, a brain area involved in learning and memory (J. Douglas Bremner, M.D et al. *2000)*. Understanding and recognizing depression and its growth potential is important to prevent social and psychological damage, as well as physical damage to the brain.

You may wonder why, of all times, depression starts to occur when things start going right for a change or you experience a sense of safety. Depression does not arrive when you feel danger or are focused on getting through the rough patches of life. You are too distracted and preoccupied with life stressors or the chaos of the family system to recognize your own needs. When you have moved beyond fear and the survival mode and have time to access some part of your true self, depression may occur. It is after the crisis that you can begin to examine who you are and what you want in life when you may expect to see depression take hold.

In this period of self-reflection when awakening of the true self and self-potential take place, internal conflict and the stalemate between the true self and the false self becomes most salient and depression is at its zenith. When self-exploration and self-understanding are freed up, people begin to realize that they have engaged in behaviors or followed a life path that is not what they want nor does it express whom they really are. They realize that where they are and who they have been up to this point in life is not who they want to continue to be forever. The true self is able to be seen with more clarity after the crisis has largely passed.

Let me give you an example. Imagine that you are driving your car down the street and suddenly you see a vehicle run a red light. It's heading straight at you. What happens? You react. You swerve, veer, and react to the danger almost instinctively. You do not think too much about it or get too emotional at that point; you just simply react. When do you notice the fear, the anxiety, and the shakiness? When do you explore the drastic possible outcomes for you and your life had the car struck you? Isn't it usually right after the incident when you have pulled to the side of the road or otherwise have reached a point of safety? It is when you feel somewhat safe or the danger has passed that you have the mental ability to reflect on what could have happened and how scary the event was.

Just as after a near collision, depression and anxiety arise when you reach a point of safety in your life and are able to wonder about what you want from life and to contemplate all the options for your future. Depression, anxiety, and discomfort all arise when, figuratively, you are pulled to the side of the road and are past the survival mode.

However, just because you have passed the survival mode and have time to reflect on your life does not mean that awareness equals reaction and forward momentum. Often time, awareness alone leads to a sense of paralysis. After a crisis, you are now free to think of all the possibilities for your life. The initial multitude of choices may be overwhelming. Deciding on a life path is fraught with choices and hesitation as you contemplate the options for your life. It is often a time when depression sets in because the prospect of embarking on a new undiscovered healthy life is almost terrifying, but so too is reverting completely to unhealthy false identities. Depression then becomes the result, as you stand immobilized at the abyss of the familiar past and the uncertainty of the future.

The same concept applies in your personal life. The more primitive the situation, the easier it is to handle because less conscious thought is given to it. The more evolved the situation, the more choices you are faced with, and the more uncertainty you experience, the more anxiety and depression you will feel in being undecided as to what direction to choose. The newer the situation, the less confidence you will have moving forward in a new direction. When someone is chasing you, you will instinctively run. There is no hesitation because you are trying to survive. When you are relaxed and options abound, you may have difficulty in deciding simple things such as what you will have for dinner that evening or wear that day.

During this time of change, people do not jump at the chance to live a more authentic and fulfilled life; it is too new and uncertain. Just as you tentatively pull your vehicle back onto the road after the near fatal collision, you will step tentatively into a new direction, but it is with frayed nerves and caution as you progress. If another car zooms by and nearly collides with you again, you may pull your car off the road again and sit there for a while or call someone to come pick you up. You are too frazzled to continue the journey. Any setback when trying to step forward quickly retriggers the behaviors of the false self and pulls you back from the true self.

After the crisis and survival mode has passed and depression is setting in is an absolutely crucial point where change can occur, if you are able to focus on the positive changes and prevent fear from taking back what the true self has gained. However, many people, during this initial stage of change upon realizing that a new path in life is unfolding for them, may not be able to endure the discomfort of starting on this new path. They may avoid change or revert to more familiar, but unhealthy, patterns to avoid the discomfort of starting over. Or, they adopt a new false persona or create some form of crisis that keeps them in a perpetual state of "survival" mode, which also keeps them from moving forward from journeying on their new path toward happiness and their true self.

To give you an example of the concepts of this chapter so far, let's use a story about Melissa, and how depression was a sign of her true self and the shedding of her false self.

Throughout high school, everything seemed fine for Melissa. She was an outgoing cheerleader, active in intramural clubs and sports, and she received almost perfect grades. Her home life was not so fine. She was victim to her older brother's rage, frequently humiliated in front of friends by his vicious verbal attacks and degrading comments about her appearance and actions. She was powerless against his relentless attacks. She would not defend herself because he would at times become physically violent to silence her protests and opinions. Melissa's mother passed away when she was four. Her father was not home very often, leaving Melissa to face the loneliness and frequent berating from her brother. On one occasion, a sexual attack from a babysitter occurred, but no one believed that it had happened. She dealt with the attack silently and alone. To make matters worse, when the father was home, he was dismissive and ignored her complaints saying only, "Your brother is in charge when I am gone. You better not cause trouble for him."

Despite the unpleasantness of her home life, she reported that during high school she experienced no signs of depression, confusion, or anxiety. Outwardly, she appeared to be the epitome of success and joviality. As an adult, Melissa was attractive, intelligent, happily married. She was finishing a Master's degree in the field of engineering.

As she approached college, she met her husband and he treated her with kindness and loved her unconditionally. He encouraged her to pursue her dreams and she became active in rugby, her favorite sport. Her husband would reinforce her intelligence, encouraging her to follow her educational interests. She began to pursue a degree in engineering and a career she had long desired. For the first time, she felt as though people really liked her for who she was. She was given the freedom to be her genuine self. Things were truly going well for her during her college years. Then Melissa began to notice her depression, the uncontrollable emotional outbursts, and the difficulty with interpersonal relations, especially with friends. After a visit with her brother one evening, she suddenly began to have frequent fights with her husband and seek constant reassurance from him that he would not leave her. She knew he loved her and would never leave her, and yet she found herself continually anxious and depressed. She simply could not explain where all these feelings came from and why now, of all times in her life, she would experience such depression and insecurity.

Why would depression come into her life now? To put it simply: because she was healing and growing. Melissa, for the first time, was beginning to experience life and interactions on her own accord that were positive. She was not subject to receiving unwarranted attacks from her brother. She was no longer expected to stifle her dreams, personality, and strengths. Rather than being forced to believe that she was powerless, useless, and insignificant, she was now encouraged and praised for her intelligence. She was with a gentle and loving man who shared her life. He was not the unattached father. He was the attached and supportive husband. She now had friends who shared her love of rugby and enjoyed time with her. She no longer had to navigate around a vicious brother, a deviant babysitter, and a removed father. She could feel love and express herself and her feelings without punishment. She was growing by feeling the unconditional acceptance from her friends and an intimate companion. She was developing her own authentic identity apart from the hurtful and powerless identity spawned during her early home life.

This new identity was unlike anything Melissa had experienced up until this time. Inside her remained the memories and identity of her past humiliating experiences. However, a new identity was emerging with each and every positive interaction with her husband, college, friends, and career success. Melissa's past learned false identity was still strong and would be retriggered and reinforced whenever she would interact with her brother. The true self was now beginning to gain strength in Melissa's adulthood, challenging the negative self-image caused by the false self, but it still was not strong enough to overshadow the false identity yet.

Melissa was beginning to struggle with her two opposing identities and two concepts of herself. She had one identity that was her genuine true self, positively reinforced in college and her marriage; the other identity operating within her was the false identity, the negative side she experienced during childhood and in early family interactions. Both of these two identities were in strong opposition now that her true self was getting more and more reinforcing feedback; both of her identities were now struggling for expression, creating uncertainty and confusion about her sense of self worth, who she was as a person, and how to interact with significant others. Her new path of the true self was unfolding and gaining strength, but with recent interactions with her brother, the false self gained strength. It increased the struggle she was feeling inside resulting in angst, depression, and some unhealthy behaviors and fears of abandonment that she played out in her home life now.

She was acting out after her recent interaction with her brother because she was at a crossroad with the old messages of the false self that were still hardwired into her mind and self-concept. The false self led her to feel and believe that she was alone in the world and her life was fraught with fears of abandonment. The other true self-identity was emerging, reinforcing the self-concept that she was loved unconditionally and worthy of love and success.

Melissa's depression began to emerge at that point because she was able to leave the chaos of her family and reduce her dependency on her false identity. Moreover, she was able to move from survival mode into one of self-reflection and self-actualization of the true self. But, the path of her true self was new and frightening. It was unknown and her fears and previous learning about abandonment remained in the back of her mind, making it difficult for her to follow the true self without hesitation. Her true self was emerging, but still not strong enough yet to overpower her entrenched false self. Therefore, not having a clear message about her sense of self and having her brother retrigger false self memories, Melissa was becoming uncertain as to what path she should choose as the true self and false self collided and depression began to arise for the first time in Melissa's life.

At a crucial point like the one Melissa faced, if a person is able to push through this time of uncertainty when the true self finds strength and expression, the depressive cycle can be broken. It does not happen with ease and it is often a time when people have short-term success only to fall back into patterns of dysfunction or recreate situations where they have to be in survival mode all over again. Unless they are well versed in their own struggle and their false self identity and behaviors, they can lose the opportunity to move forward in life. Instead, they adopt a continuous cycle of survival mode to keep them from experiencing the discomfort of engaging in a new path. It's like starting any new behavior—riding a bike, typing, learning a new computer program or job skill. It is difficult at first, but with time and practice, it eventually becomes as natural as walking.

Without effective strategies to help with change, some people cannot endure the uncertainty that comes with moving away from the false self. They sabotage themselves or aspects of their lives. People with the invisible persona, explosive persona, and the super-producer persona fall back into survival mode to feel the familiar once again, rather than push forward into an area of growth and the experience of their true self.

For the invisible persona, you may see someone with a horrific domestic violence abuse history return to the abuser or find another unhealthy relationship. In a super-producer persona, you may see the person taking on additional tasks or hours at work just when the family starts to grow closest and most connected. The explosive persona may start drinking or putting himself/herself into situations where a bar fight or other legal action may occur when he/she has had months of sobriety, possibly started a new job or otherwise has life back on track.

Whatever the case and whatever the false identity persona, the result is that the person who is in survival mode continuously is left with nothing other than repetition or escalation of previous unhealthy relationship patterns and unhealthy behaviors. Unless a person can recognize how uncomfortable emotional states, such as depression, are a sign of growth and have techniques for helping to endure the emergence of the true self, that person can get stuck in replaying survival to avoid growth.

You would think that people would naturally gravitate towards events or situations where happiness could be found, but this is not the case for those that have strong false identities. The false identity can be so powerful that when the true self emerges, the person may feel that it is not genuine or that they may not deserve the success or happiness that comes along with it. They may feel that eventually the happiness or goodness that exists in their life will be lost or taken away from them. It always had been taken away before, so they do things to force the failure of success, happiness, or family harmony.

Some people that have experienced chaotic situations early in life, with strong hardwired false identities, never allow themselves to feel safe. They continue to create "unsafe" conditions within their lives or relationships. There is a fear that whatever gains they make will be lost, and that letting go of the familiar survival mode and false identity for an unexplored authentic or true identity will result in a greater sense of loss and unhappiness. They may repeatedly sabotage their lives, family, or jobs to stay in survival mode because it is more familiar and keeps them from experiencing a greater sense of loss in the future when their guard is down. They create a survival mode as an emotional armor to prevent themselves from feeling vulnerable.

A person who falls back into survival mode and resists growth is commonly without support. Many people try to avoid the myriad choices in life. They avoid finding out who they are and what they really want from life because it does not come without depression, uncertainty, and some anxiety symptoms.

For many, emotional states such as depression, anxiety, vulnerability, and sadness are more difficult to endure than it is to continue with past unhealthy behaviors or situations, even if the old situations involve prospects for physical violence. People sometimes will choose to sabotage their life direction to stay in the survival mode and limit their emotional experiences to anger. People may experience a mid life crisis or engage in affairs, addictive or destructive behaviors such as drinking when they can no longer tolerate being far from survival mode and fear the uncertainty of the true self life path.

People who force themselves back into survival mode can become work-a-holics and start avoiding intimacy with family and friends, all in an attempt to have friction that leads to survival mode. You may see a father suddenly start isolating himself from his children or his wife, spending more time with his buddies, more time drinking, engaging in hobbies to excess, or becoming suddenly aggressive or jealous just after he has accomplished things or reached a plateau in his life.

You may see people who struggled in their lives to achieve money, success, or fame only to needlessly throw it all away and begin engaging in reckless and self-destructive behaviors after they have achieved the successful goal they have sought for themselves. You see this in many celebrities like Britney Spears who was at the top of her game and suddenly started sabotaging her career and making public displays of self-damning gestures like cutting her hair off or public intoxication. You may see a stay-at-home mother begin to flirt with idea of an affair when her home life seems comfortable and safe.

Whatever your true identity and true self may be, it will eventually come out and fight with the false self when the survival mode is suppressed. Staying in the survival mode is something that cannot last forever if a person is receiving some positive feedback from the true self. Many people try to force it to remain by artificially creating friction or failure in life. The greater the power of the false self, the greater the destructive behaviors when the true self combats it. If the person has significant pull from both sides of the true self and the false self, the more destructive the battle will be for the person and his/her life.

As we age, we get tired and have a harder time forcing the survival mode and suppressing the true self. The formerly distant father may try to rekindle a relationship with a child. The cheating spouse may try to reignite the connection of a past marriage promising no more infidelity. Or the true self may be subtle where one may start having fantasies of opening a charity, traveling, or doing something different with his/her life and character. The celebrity may announce that he/she is done with show business. The successful businessperson may sell everything and move to Africa to start a charitable organization. Whatever the true self dictates, the stronger the true self, the weaker the false self will become if it is not reinforced. The energy of the true self will find ways to express itself as we receive positive feedback in our life, or as we age and lose the emotional and physical strength required to stay in survival mode. It will be harder and harder to suppress the internal struggle between the false self and the true self if both are reinforced, but less of a struggle if one is significantly reinforced over the other.

You, just as Melissa and others have, will prosper by exploring the underlying and sustaining motivators for your behaviors, distress, depression, and/or anxiety. By adopting new techniques for honoring your true genuine self, by being aware of what you are putting out into the world, and changing maladaptive behavioral patterns, you will reawaken your potential for growth and sustainable happiness. We will say more on techniques for behavioral and verbal changes in later chapters. For now, we will focus on helping you discover your own personal struggle and see the sustaining forces behind your false persona.

Chapter Four

Discovering Your Inner Struggle

"Some cannot loosen their own chains but can nonetheless redeem their friends."

-NIETZSCHE-

To discover your own struggle, you must first be aware of your role within your family and understand how that role contributed to maintaining the balance in the family. Although we have discussed much of this in previous chapters, not everyone is even aware that they are locked in some kind of internal struggle from early family interactions. It is much easier to see the struggles of others than it is to discover the difficulties within ourselves. In fact, many people arrange their lives so that they never have to look at their own struggles or at how the past has redirected their lives.

On the surface, many people may seem productive, well adjusted, and perhaps perfectly content while they suffer silently inside. They may have the *super-producer persona* where in social situations they thrive and take care of multiple tasks for everyone. However, when they are alone and without tasks to distract themselves from the internal distress, they are miserable and suffering in silence.

The first step toward change is simple awareness of your struggle and identification of your path. This chapter will help you to become aware of your own personal history and the family system imbalance that may have caused you to adopt a false persona. Although awareness is the first step toward happiness and emotional stability, it is also the most difficult step because many people subconsciously keep from looking at their struggle because growth is not without discomfort. They do this not because they choose misery, but because they choose to look away from their own struggle. Confrontation and acknowledgement is at times emotionally painful.

By ignoring your personal struggle, it is only short-term gain with long-term consequences. In the short-term, by ignoring it and adopting distracting behaviors or false personas, it keeps you from experiencing the unpleasant emotions that are waging inside between the true self and false self. It also keeps you from engaging in life on a deeper and more fulfilling level. Ignoring the personal struggle keeps depression and anxiety lingering because the emotions are trapped inside and continually suppressed by our coping skills and will. Only by first becoming aware of the emotional struggle inside and feeling the discomfort of depression and anxiety will you be able to move beyond the false identity and move into a realm of growth towards the attainment of the true self.

As we touched on in previous chapters, sometimes we find unhealthy ways to distract ourselves from feeling uncomfortable emotions. Other times, we find healthy ways of temporarily distracting ourselves such as through social engagements, sports, or intensive exercise regimens. However, in the long run, the depression and anxiety return in cycles because we have not understood what sustains the unpleasant emotions nor have we given ourselves room to allow our true identity to be realized and expressed. We cannot keep distractions going forever because we get exhausted over time. Eventually we get physically tired and have to face the unpleasant emotions that we have tried so hard to push away. Like shaking a soda bottle, the longer we fight to ignore the struggle, the greater the pressure will build until one day everything comes spewing out in disastrous and damaging ways.

When it comes to understanding your own personal struggle and the factors that are sustaining self-defeating behaviors, beliefs, or negative emotions such as depression and anxiety, we have to look at who you are, who you were expected to be by others, and your overall experience growing up. However, looking at the past is not about blame. This book is not intended for you to find a scapegoat for personal difficulties. Looking at the past helps you to see how your family system tried to achieve balance and how that weight may have been unfairly placed on one family member more than another.

As I said earlier, all family systems essentially seek to find balance; not all go about it in the most productive way. Looking at the past is a way to see how you personally tried to rectify the imbalance of the system and how those behaviors impact you today.

Not only do we have to look at how our past shaped or influenced our identity and supports our false identities, we have to look at our own current contributions and behaviors that may be reinforcing our early learned false identities. We have to examine what behaviors we are engaging in, and what beliefs we hold about our core self-worth. We have to thoroughly examine the current behaviors that are further sustaining the learned behaviors of our past. We will explore what we are doing, consciously or unconsciously, through our communication that is inadvertently aligning our environment to our own internal false identities and self-beliefs. In later chapters, we will discuss how simple things, such as the language we use, determine and influence people during our social interaction.

For the moment, we will spend some time on examining other influences that impair our ability to understand our own struggle and make lasting changes. Some of the major obstacles that people face when it comes to recognizing struggles are simply the demands of daily life.

Those that have the super-producer personas and those that have had significant socio-cultural disadvantages have faced life in a continual survival mode. Many of those from impoverished and/or abusive households simply have not had the opportunity to examine who they are and what they may want for their life. Many that have faced difficult or demanding life situations such as becoming teenage parents, being on their own at an early age, coming from severely impoverished homes, or any other situations where survival was a daily struggle, have had little time for self-exploration and self-awareness. The demands of daily life have precluded the self-examination of their struggle because so many are dependent on their action-oriented behaviors. They are locked in survival mode because they actually are responsible for survival for themselves or for others in their family.

In these cases, growth cannot begin until situations improve or they are able to step aside from the chaotic daily routine and begin a brief examination of behaviors and their direction in life. For those that are locked into survival mode, such as in a severely violent domestic relationship, there can be no progress until a place of safety can be reached. Sometimes, leaving the environment or finding additional outside support through a state agency, church, or extended family members may be necessary before any progress can commence.

When people have attained a place of basic safety, they can look at their own life and struggle, examine their own level of current happiness, and clearly project into the future what direction they would like for their life path. Only then will it give a better clue as to their own struggle and how to change it.

For those that may be at a loss to identify their own struggle, or for those that may experience resistance when it comes to examining their own behaviors, a quick step toward understanding the struggle is by simply looking at how you try to change others. This is an easy exercise for revealing to some degree your internal struggles.

Looking at what you dislike in others can give you a clue about your own struggle between your true and false self. The behaviors of others may elicit more intense emotions or efforts on your part than the actions of those perpetrating the actions may warrant. For example, you may be the best advisor for others' relationships, but are embroiled in disastrous relationships yourself. You may dislike clutter and place unrealistic demands on your spouse for cleanliness because early on you may have been exposed to a chaotic an unpredictable environment. Clutter could be an outward manifestation of that chaos.

Take a moment and examine the behaviors you are trying to change in others or what bothers you most in other people. Look at the qualities in people that annoy you, and see if any of those behaviors are found within yourself or within your early life environment.

If you expect no changes of others, take a moment and think about the direction of your life. Where will you end up if your current life path and direction continues? Is that the direction you feel is correct for you? If not, the struggle is revealed in the difference between your current life and the life you would like for yourself. If you realize in projecting your current life path into the future that you would keep engaging in destructive behaviors or that you would continue giving emotionally to people only to have it never returned, then you have a clue as to what the struggle is for you. You may become aware that an invisible persona is operating within your own life. It's time to explore your own role within the family and see if it aligns with your true self or if life has imposed a false identity on you.

EFFECTS OF THE PAST; HOW YOUR OWN STRUGGLE DEVELOPED

It requires courage to look at sensitive areas, painful mistakes and memories, and to decide upon committing to change in your life. There will be natural resistance to acknowledging your own contributions and those of others to your own unhappiness. It is sometimes easier to blame others for our failings or mistakes than it is to acknowledge that they are our mistakes alone. In future chapters, we touch on how blaming others can often happen in relationships and can keep us from changing our destructive patterns when we blame others without looking at our own contributions.

After you have taken a moment to realize that some form of an emotional struggle exists for you, it is important to see how it developed, what keeps it alive, how it plays out in daily interactions and behaviors, and how you and others sustain that struggle with behaviors. Initially understanding your struggle begins by going back to explore your past just as we have done with Melissa from the previous example. We have thoroughly explored how the past and early family and social interactions can either negatively or positively influence your personality.

Again, exploring the past is not meant to identify a scapegoat for responsibility. Exploring the past is a way to understand how you have adapted to the world you were exposed to and how you may have deviated from your true self in trying to find family harmony. The past is not something we can change, so you may wonder why you should bother looking back when all you want to do is to change your future.

When we only look forward, we tend to repeat our behaviors that led us astray in the first place. We tend to repeat our mistakes and end up traveling down the same path that took us away from our potential. If we try to navigate forward by the use of a faulty map, we only end up lost in life. We must look back to develop a clear direction for our life and future. By looking into the past, it serves as a polestar for us to see and understand why and how we have forged this life's path. We see where we are now because we clearly see our starting direction. The past helps you to understand how the false persona developed and how you can minimize its impact on your future direction.

Examining the past helps make a permanent change instead of simply making minor switchbacks and deviations. For example, leaving one bad relationship is a temporary fix if you continue to have a pattern of attracting and being attracted to the same type of person that resulted in bad relationships in the first place. When you go back to explore why you are attracted to that type of person to begin with, you can teach yourself to avoid unhealthy relationships and understand what you are gaining from the pursuit of unhealthy relationships.

By thoroughly exploring your identity, how others were instrumental in shaping your self-view and identity, and what behaviors keep you on your current troubled path, you will have a better chance to sustain the growth when you initiate changes in your life.

Think back to when you were growing up. How did you come to discover who you were and how you learned about the world around you? Your family, your friends, your teachers, your coaches, or any other adult or person involved in your life were all powerful influences on how you came to see yourself. Their feedback, comments, praise, criticisms, spankings, hugs, or any other interaction that they may have had with you gave you feedback on your importance to them and your importance to the world. Each interaction you experienced early on began the hardwiring of your mind. You learned through the messages they gave you about how they saw you and how each behavior you engaged in was met with reward or punishment.

Consistently, if a teacher praises a child for his/her efforts by saying, "You have done a great job," or "you are very bright," then you could see how a child could develop a strong sense of self-efficacy that strengthens the true self. On the other hand, if the teacher says, "you have done a horrible job," or "you are stupid," then you could easily see how a child could develop a negative sense of self even if the negative information the teacher provided was not factual.

Your peers, family, and other early social interactions are mirrors reflecting the way you will see yourself. If the feedback significant others provided you is positive and you are given the opportunity to test your limits, fail without punishment, and succeed with recognition, then your esteem and sense of your true self is enhanced. The more positive feedback you receive from your efforts to explore yourself and the world, the stronger your sense of self becomes.

However, when your significant others or attachment figures (parents, siblings, coaches, teachers, etc) begin to criticize, punish or avoid providing basic safety, affection, and trust, then their negative feedback on your self-worth begins to impact the way you see yourself. Significantly. The impact of negative feedback early on is one of the most powerful forces for shaping your future and sense of self.

IMPACT OF NEGATIVE FEEDBACK

When it comes to negative feedback and early learning, the more derisive and negative the message is and the longer the negative feedback is provided, the more devastating the results are for stifling the true sense of self within you. Even if there is some occasional positive feedback administered during this time, the negative feedback far outweighs the positive. One negative comment can offset as much as twenty positive comments (Markman, Stanley, Blumberg 2001). So imagine the devastating effects of years of negative feedback and unhealthy messages about your identity and your place in the world. Think how easily a false identity can develop with such powerful impact from negative statements. Imagine how many positive interactions it would take later in life to offset all the negative feedback. The number is sometimes astronomical.

To bring this concept home, imagine that a child heard one simple negative comment every day for ten years. In those ten years, that would mean that child would have heard three thousand six hundred fifty negative messages (3,650). Since one negative comment offsets twenty positive statements, that would mean that the child would have to have been given over seventy-three thousand positive statements (73,000) to prevent damage of the negative feedback. To understand the enormity of this, the child would have to be given nearly one positive feedback nearly every hour, every day, for close to ten straight years to offset the one negative comment given each day for the ten years! Now imagine if the child is from an abusive background or a home with domestic violence. Imagine how large the number of incidents for positive feedback would have to be to offset the damage given ten to fifteen negative comments per day over ten years!

With numbers like that, you can see how easy it is to be influenced by a negative self-concept and how easily a false identity can form. With every passing interaction, the body and mind stores images and memories of these interactions, sometimes consciously, and other times subconsciously, as implicit memories. Regardless of how they are stored, conscious or unconscious, the memories are stored and are triggered with various interactions in life. Some part of you always remembers this identity, past negative experience, and feedback. You retain vestiges of this false identity in neuropathways and neural connections. Some evidence of this vestigial negative self-view is evident in every word you say and every move you make to some degree. We will discuss how your language and non-verbal cues may be reinforcing this past negative identity in more depth in later chapters.

For now, let it suffice that the early identity is stored within you like a computer program. If the program is unadulterated or untainted by viruses and corrupt files, then things operate smoothly. However, if negative feedback is given and it outweighs the positive, then the negative identity and memories become like the virus in a computer corrupting the operation of the computer. The virus may lay in wait until something triggers the virus or memories to spread and corrupt the operating system.

The frequent free expression of your true self and receiving positive feedback to offset the negative information can help to "clean" the virus from our memories. However, as we have discussed above, it will take many positive interactions to offset the negative early learning experiences.

The more positive feedback you receive over time, the more offset the negative information provided you early in life, and the more dormant the virus will be. As you grow older, your world grows beyond family to include colleagues, significant others, peers, friends, and other social interactions that may promote the positive aspects of your identity and self. However, after years of learning negative feedback, sometimes the viruses have been planted too deeply and this negative sense of self remains a part of us even when we feel positive about our life and our self.

Like flexing a muscle, keeping the negative sense of self or the false self at bay requires effort and is exhausting if the early learning existed for a long period of time. The slightest negative interaction can trigger the virus to be activated and spread to hinder your accurate view of yourself, the future, and the world later in life. The *kindling model of depression* states that thinking negative thoughts can have effects on the increased sensitivity in activation of neural structures which then will increase the likelihood that depression and other negative mood states will occur more easily in the future (Segal, et al, 1996).

No matter how perfect our interactions are growing up, we all have some emotional and negative "viruses" inside, some more pernicious than others. We all have experienced ourselves as both good and bad and have received feedback from significant others, family, co-workers, and others accordingly. We have insecurity issues around a topic due to our feedback and past. We all have received feedback in two dimensions—positive and negative—throughout our lives. In effect, our experiences in life build up and are stored in an accurate sense of self when we receive positive feedback and interactions with others and an inaccurate self when we receive unhealthy feedback from others. In a few moments, we will have you look at your own history, but let's examine one more example to clarify the information thus far and how dormant early learning can impact positive situations later in life.

EXAMPLE:

Barry is a young father, happily married for ten years, and a successful insurance broker. He began to notice that he has been talking with more women, openly flirting with them and on two occasions, has offered to take women on dates. He noticed that he has become depressed, irritable, and moody with his kids.

We began to explore his life and discovered how early on he was told he would amount to nothing. His father was an aggressive man who would drink more than appropriate on occasion. On these occasions, he would berate Barry and call him worthless, telling him he would amount to nothing. Growing up, when Barry would fail in school, his mother and father would berate him for ten minutes on what a poor student he was. When he did well, he was often ignored and his parents frequently invalidated his attempts to reach out to them for positive praise on his school efforts. In essence, the parents only provided attention when Barry failed or did something wrong. Even if the attention is punishment, it was attention nonetheless. When Barry succeeded, it was as if he did not exist. His parents paid little if any attention to his success.

As Barry grew into adolescence, he noticed that he was attracted to the rebel type of women that would emotionally and physically exploit him. He was angry and lashed out frequently with friends and lovers. After a few run-ins with the law, Barry eventually went to college where he found a passion for business and excelled in school with honors. He additionally met a caring young woman whom he later married. Barry's efforts in college earned him recognition and praise from the Dean and helped land him land a lucrative job right out of college. Barry lost the dangerous rebel side, and *found pride in his school and work accomplishments. Years after college, Barry now has a happy marriage and a successful career.*

One day, while at work, Barry was called into the office. He had made a serious but simple mistake and was berated by his boss who'd had a bad day and overreacted to Barry's mistake. A few days later, Barry noticed that he felt moody, depressed, and began to pick arguments with his wife. He began to become more irritable with the kids and the moodiness continued for a few months without him understanding why. Barry began to grow distant and reckless at work and started to entertain the idea of infidelity. He openly flirted with women. Why did this minor incident at work send Barry into a tailspin?

Let's look back at Barry's life. In the beginning as a child, he was given a painful and inaccurate message about himself and his self worth. He would pursue relationships with women that treated him as his parents had, further reinforcing his negative sense of self. Barry would receive feedback, although negative feedback, when he failed and was told he was a failure. However, somewhere along the line, enough of his true identity emerged that he was able to attend college and, through positive feedback from teachers and bosses, he was able to see himself with a positive self worth more clearly.

He stopped seeing women that treated him poorly and exploited him. He was able to see that he deserved better than to be overlooked and trampled on by others and soon married. However, the identity that he formed early on still stayed with him, dormant, waiting in the shadows for an opportunity to reemerge. His supervisor (a man in position of power) offered harsh criticism about his work, re-triggering the false self. The reckless Barry and the "failure" identity emerged once again with one strong incident of criticism from his boss.

Like pushing on a bruise, the combination of criticism and a male in power (father figure) triggered a flood of past events and awakened Barry's sleeping false identity. Barry was not completely subjected to his false self. He had received enough positive feedback in his marriage and college years that his true self was able to combat the false self somewhat. Barry was able to identify his behaviors and to argue with his false identity and negative behaviors as he would openly say, "It's silly that I feel this way," yet the depression persisted.

A silent struggle waged inside of Barry. There was a conflict between the vulnerable little boy and that of the competent man and father. Even though the information for Barry's positive sense of self-worth was overwhelming, the memories and feelings of vulnerability still remained and overrode the more recent positive identity. Some memories, called implicit memories, are memories that are stored viscerally without conscious awareness and can be triggered easily by subtle reminders of the event with powerful emotional responses. For example, if a traumatic event happened in a dark alleyway, simply walking by a dark alleyway will re-trigger the powerful emotions you experienced on that day even if you consciously were not aware of seeing an alleyway. This happens in many situations where Post Traumatic Stress Disorder originated. The domineering boss triggered these implicit memories, unleashing the false identities and hardwired memories of long ago that impacted Barry's behaviors and present conduct.

Now let us get back to your struggle. It's time to construct your short story and identify precisely your struggle and your True Self and False Self. Take a few moments to either write it out or simply think about your life. Begin with your earliest memories and think of your life as if you were writing about someone else right up to the point to where you are now.

Now, after you write out or think about your story, write out ten incidents below that really impacted you negatively. Write out times when you felt rejected, embarrassed, or were made to see yourself and your place in the world in a negative way. By looking at your past interactions and exploring them from an outside perspective, you can begin to understand why you may react to criticism, rejection, and being alone. *Please be cautious as you write about your past and if you are not ready to delve into these memories, do not begin this exercise or speak with your therapist about what these memories may trigger before you begin this exercise.* Write out some of your significant memories. These should be memories of events, interactions and memories that evoked powerful feelings. Use the following spaces to write out all ten. If you have trouble thinking of them, take your time until all ten are completed.

Your story:
Write out the 10 negative incidents below.

1) _____

2) _____

3) _____

4) _____

5) _____

6) _____

7) _____

8) _____

9) _____

10) _____

After you have completed the ten or so scenarios above, visualize a young child (visualize a boy if you are male, or a girl if you are a female) sitting across from you in a chair looking at you. Imagine looking into his/her eyes. Think of looking at a little child that lived that story and experienced all the things above and answer four questions:

1. **How would that child feel about himself/herself?**

2. **How readily would that child accept positive feedback from others?**

3. **Given only the situations above, what would the child's life/ future be like?**

4. **Without these incidents, what would the child's future and direction be?**

Understand that that child described above is *you*, and how you responded to the first three questions above is the false identity that remains within you competing with the true sense of self. The fourth question is the positive and true sense of yourself, the nurturing, compassionate side that helps you to offer positive feedback to yourself and the world. The first three questions are derived from your past, and the fourth is derived from your potential to change your future.

The past is a powerful contributor to the way we see our learned behaviors and our self. When we continue to see our lives through the eyes

Discovering Your Inner Struggle

of a child, we do not see the situations and ourselves accurately. We do not have the capacity to stand up for ourselves against powerful parental figures, dominating authority figures, or unhealthy significant others. We accept the feedback unquestioningly and may come to see ourselves as the problem. But that is not an accurate perception of our past.

Let's look at how to reconstruct your past and reconstruct your true identity. Take the time to think of the positive interactions or situations where you felt loved, respected, fulfilled, and/or acknowledged. Write out some of your significant memories. Think of a time when family, friends, and loved ones really seemed to understand you and you felt the interaction was meaningful to you on a healthy and positive level.

Write out the positive incidents below.

1)_____

2)_____

3)_____

4)_____

5)_____

6)_____

7)_____

8)_____

9)_____

10)_____

After you have completed the ten or so scenarios above, do the same thing as you did above. Visualize a young child (visualize a boy if you are male, or a girl if you are female) sitting across from you in a chair looking at you. Think of looking at a little child that experienced all the things above and answer four questions:

1. How would that child feel about himself/herself?

___

2. How readily would that child accept positive feedback from others?

___

3. Given only the situations above, what would the child's life/ future be like?

___

4. How would your future be if these positive interactions continued to reaffirm who you are?

___

How you feel when doing this exercise is the real you, and it is waiting for further discovery and expression. Understand that no matter how many negative incidents and negative situations you have experienced in your life, they can be overcome and overwritten by positive feedback with sufficient time and practice. Although there may still be some vestigial elements of early learning, with practice and patience, the false self can be overshadowed by the true self.

You need to practice internally by changing your self-talk as well as externally by identifying your behaviors and removing yourself from unhealthy environments that may reinforce the false self. Many people try to seek external validation while internally delivering the same negative messages they received growing up. They may seek validation through relationships, accomplishments, etc. while all along filling their minds with words of self-doubt and negative statements.

When you change the internal negative messages, you begin to offset the negative external messages. You communicate more with yourself than you do with others. Indirectly and directly, you provide feedback to yourself literally thousands of times per day. By changing your beliefs, behaviors, and thoughts, you can quickly provide positive and automatic authentic reinforcing messages thousands of times per day. In the next chapter, we will explore how the mind at times can be your best ally or your worst enemy when it comes to actualizing your potential for becoming who you are.

Chapter Five

Why Your Brain Can Be Your Worst Enemy Or Your Best Ally

"Our life is what our thoughts make it."
-Marcus Aurelius Antoninus-

When we have difficulty changing our unhealthy or maladaptive behaviors, we can oftentimes be very hard on ourselves. The smoker may berate himself when he is unable to quit smoking; the woman chides herself when she keeps dating the same type of unhealthy guy; parents becomes depressed because they are unable to communicate with their children and express the emotions they really feel inside.

Whatever the behaviors we want to see changed, it is simply not that easy to change them after we have engaged in them over a long period of time. We cannot simply flip a switch and change our behaviors without some residual resistance from our past learning. Change takes time and repetition due to the hardwiring of our neural pathways and neural connections that we develop over time with repeated behaviors.

Changing any behavior or interpersonal interaction that you have repeated over years is difficult initially because you are battling with your brain. It has little to do with your willpower alone. The more you have engaged in certain behaviors, the greater the neural connections and the larger the neural pathways that make those behaviors easier with less conscious thought. When you first learned to drive a car, your hands were at ten and two, your anxiety levels were high, and you had all of your attention focused on the task of driving. After years of driving, you now have to think little of the multiple decisions you make with every mile of driving. With enough driving experience, you learn to multitask. You can sing, adjust the radio, and talk on your hands free cell phone all while navigating the roads effortlessly. Your mind learned the ability to drive so effectively that you give it little conscious thought.

The same applies with any learned behaviors from your past, whether they are productive or destructive. Initially, they require effort but become so automatic that you may not even notice that you are engaged in them at all. When you decide to change a behavior that is driven by a false self, the neural connections for a new behavior are not as strong as those for the old and established behaviors. Consequently, it is extremely difficult to prevent yourself from falling back into old behaviors if the new ones are not practiced frequently. Willpower alone will not suffice to permanently fix unhealthy behaviors no matter how badly you want to see change in your life and your behaviors. It takes time and frequent repetition before the new behaviors can correct or hold back the behaviors from the established false identities and capitalize on the strength of your will.

Let me give you an example. Let's say that an unhealthy learned behavior is a giant ship. You want to stop these behaviors, so you try to learn a new behavior. The new behavior attempts to tether the massive ship to a dock. When you first engage in a new behavior that is trying to offset the previous learning, it is as if a thread is holding the ship to the dock because the neuropathways are not developed yet. Just a little nudge is required for the ship to pull from the dock and snap the thread-sized tether. However, if every day, new threads were added to the single tether, eventually the single thread would become a giant rope holding the ship firmly to the dock. Pulling your ship away from the dock now would not be as easy as it was in the beginning because the combined strength of the threads make it a solid rope. With behaviors, the newer and less practiced they are, the weaker the neuropathways until repetition allows you to develop strong and multiple neural connections to prevent unhealthy behaviors from driving your behaviors.

With daily practice of a new behavior, change will occur over time. Each time you engage in it, another thread is added to the growing rope. The change has to be more than simple behaviors alone. Changing just outward behaviors is helpful but is not sufficient to make lasting change and turn that thread into rope. You will have to change the way you see yourself, think about yourself, and be aware of how you communicate with others to impact the way in which they engage with you to make lasting change. Without changing the way you see yourself from the inside, no matter what you do, change will be at best brief and superficial.

As they try to change behaviors and negative self-beliefs, people will change jobs, partners, even move to different states or countries thinking that physical changes will make things better, only to find that whatever they are running from begins again wherever they are. People always take the one thing with them that they have not changed—themselves.

Without conscious recognition, you shape the external world to match your internal world and internal self-construct in subtle and not so subtle ways. With each interaction, you not only interpret the information based on how you see yourself and your self-worth, you also send messages into the world about how you expect people to view you, interact with you, and ultimately like or dislike you. Subtle messages you have been giving yourself or those given to you by others are now being outwardly projected to whomever you interact with. You *project* the false identity now to your external world through subtle or not so subtle verbal and non-verbal communication.

INTERNALIZED PROJECTIONS; REVEALING THE VOICE OF THE FALSE SELF

To elaborate this point, let us explore a false identity of the *invisible persona* and the thoughts and behaviors that reinforce that false identity. Let's say that you had to be the shy, quiet type to avoid a domineering parent or sibling. After years of learning how to "hide" yourself from the world, your brain has adopted a false identity where hiding is paramount. Your thoughts will now reinforce that invisible persona. When in a social situation, your brain will begin to think things like, "I don't want to say anything because people may get mad or not like me." Or your brain may reinforce avoidant behaviors such as when a person comes up to say hello, you look away and talk little to the person, finding any excuse to leave the social situation. The person gets the impression that you do not want to talk and steps away essentially avoiding you and reinforcing your negative beliefs stemming from the false self. Your brain has so efficiently adopted the false persona that even once outside the unhealthy environment that created it, the invisible persona still operates to where you begin to create the invisible persona in new social situations to reinforce your negative beliefs and expectations of failure.

Let's look at your automatic beliefs and the voice of the false self. Think back to either this morning or yesterday morning when you first woke up and looked into the mirror. When you stood there staring at yourself and your body, what were your first thoughts? Did you smile and say positive remarks? Or did you avert your gaze and mutter silent statements of disgust at the person staring back at you within the glass? When someone offers you a compliment, do you smile and say "thank you" or do you look away and say some comment to discount the compliment?

When you look in the mirror, your mind will automatically make comments to your subconscious mind and you will alter your behavior based on this automatic self-talk. Your mind is sometimes devious and you will make silent negative comments, show certain body language, or make gestures without being aware of it. Some people avoid looking in the mirror because they do not like what they see. If you cannot look at yourself, how do you think you are projecting your self-image to others and what message are you sending about your self-worth and how others should treat you? If you cannot treat yourself well, why would others treat you differently? People will treat you in the same way you treat yourself. People will view you the same way you view yourself.

We all have good and bad days, but subtle self-messages give you feedback about the world and your interactions with it. The internal voice either gives you kudos for success or highlights the failures along with negative self-commentary. Whether successful or not, your internal voice and self-perspective will alter your actions, verbalizations, and body language that others will perceive and respond to.

If you say to yourself, "I feel fat, ugly, and I should lose weight," or "What a loser" as you look in the mirror, you have done nothing but reinforce the negative perceptions and false self. What's worse is that the more you say it each time you look in the mirror, the more conditioned and automatic the negative thoughts will become and the more you will project this negative self view into the environment. Again, you are reinforcing the neuropathways for negative self-perceptions. After a while, the mere reflection of your image will bring about feelings of despair, despondency, or even disgust without any conscious thought.

Without knowing it, you may make comments throughout the day to coworkers and friends about the way you view yourself. Subtly, you are reinforcing the negative perception within them that you are "fat," "ugly," "insecure," or not worth their time. When you feel confident, you project positive messages and people pick up on the positive energy or message that you are putting out.

Whatever message you are putting out into the world, others begin to view you by that image. People respond to and act towards you in whatever way you are projecting. When negative identities are operating, negative messages are being conveyed. To allow room for your true self to be expressed, you will need to explore how the internal dialogue you have with yourself influences the external dialogue you have with others and alters their interactions towards you.

Let's examine how your words and self-statements may be revealing your negative internal views and shaping the world around you:

Meta-Messages; the Meaning Behind the Words
Explore these common sentences:
1. *"I always screw things up!"*
2. *"How stupid was I for doing that?"*
3. *"You must really dislike me, right?"*

Let's break these sentences down and look at how unwittingly you are "programming" others to respond to your internal self-beliefs and false identity.

With every sentence or spoken word there is what is known as a **meta-message.** A meta-message is a term coined by Gerard Nierenberg (1973) referring to the message behind the direct communication, similar to a connotation. However, a meta-message is less overt than direct communication. It is an energy or subconscious message that you convey when you are communicating. Have you ever listened to someone say things like, "everything's fine" when in actuality they were angry or upset? You knew they were angry but the direct communication, the content, was that they were doing fine. You may have felt perplexed and frustrated by the conflicting communication. You may be doing this type of conflicting communication yourself or showing other forms of communication that are reinforcing the negative message or false self without even knowing it.

We all convey meta-messages in every sentence we speak. When false identities are operating, the meta-messages are picked up intuitively and shape the way people view us and interact with us. The meta-messages can be contained in body language, facial expression, tone of voice, or even in a simple "feeling" or "energy." It is more intuitive than understanding. Let's explore the meta-messages from the sentences cited above to help you understand your meta-messages.

The first sentence was, "*I always screw things up!*" The meta-message is "*I am angry at myself and I deserve to be treated poorly.*" When someone receives this type of message from you, they are likely to approach you with a mild form of hostility and reproach. Think of a time when you have uttered this statement and recall the responses from those around you. Even if those around you are trying to deliver a positive statement back to you when you make this self-deprecating statement, the tone with which they deliver this statement may seem unconvincing or perhaps even punitive. They may say to you, "*Don't say things like that!*" or "*You're crazy!*" "*Why do you say things like that? That's awful of you to say.*" When you utter such self-depreciatory comments, it sends the message that you will not stand up for yourself and it triggers others to act with hostility because they are responding to the meta-message from your internalized negative self-concept.

Having a negative self-concept and low self-esteem as is often found in an invisible persona can be less overt in your communication as well. Rather than having someone make negative self-statements, they can simply dismiss positive ones with the same self-depreciatory or dismissive outcome from others. For example, if someone compliments you, you may feel uncomfortable, and dismiss it quickly. Positive praise brings with it a mild discomfort because, at the core, you do not believe positively about yourself and positive statements you receive from others are counter to your own self-view. You will not only reject the positive from others, you will project the same message of negative self view and discomfort when you praise others and subconsciously withhold positive meta-message about yourself because it is at odds with your self-concept.

Even if someone's words are presented in such a way that they are trying to be encouraging, the tone with which they deliver the words may feel punitive because your meta-message was asking for punitive feedback. Believe positive messages about yourself and you will carry meta-messages to help others to reinforce that positive sense of self.

All communication is laden with meta-messages. Have you ever asked to help someone but that person turned you down, yet somehow you felt guilty for not helping? You are responding to their meta-message of asking for help even though their verbal message is denying assistance. Many arguments begin because the meta-message is in opposition to the verbal response and the one on the receiving end is confused, conflicted, and frustrated by the inconsistencies of meta-messages and direct verbal messages. The meta-messages will take precedence over the contextual or words themselves.

The second sentence in the example above is, *"How stupid was I for doing that?"* People have been trained to answer questions when one is posed. When you pose a rhetorical question like the one above, you trigger people to respond. People may not have thought about your actions as stupid until you posed the question triggering their thinking to process the interaction and give feedback on your premise of being stupid. The meta-message is, *"I already know I was stupid so you can tell me I was stupid"* so people respond and accommodate your wish. Their responses only further your negative self-concept and may cause you to see your actions with more negativity than you yourself initially saw.

Let's say you made a mistake at work and you make the statement, *"How stupid was I for doing that?"* You are likely to get the response, *"Yeah, that was pretty dumb. What were you thinking?"* because you planted the suggestion that your act was stupid or negative. Had you responded to the mistake by saying, *"That was a learning experience and I will do better the next time,"* you have removed the negative suggestion. You are likely to hear more positive responses like, *"It's no big deal. I am sure you will do better next time."* People offer encouragement when you encourage yourself and offer criticism when you criticize yourself.

The third and final example is, *"You must really dislike me, right?"* This is a particularly powerful sentence because although we are seeking contrary feedback to being disliked, we have inadvertently sent a meta-message in the form of a command. The simple word of *"must"* is a command statement with no room for options. When you say, *"You must dislike me"* it is internalized as *"You must dislike me!"* Many verbal messages we deliver have words with no options or alternatives such as *"must," "have to," "always," "continuously,"* etc.

When you provide sentences with these qualifiers, the receiver of the message may begin to experience discomfort when they try to counteract the statement you issued. Some may say, *"No, I don't dislike you,"* but it is less convincing than if you had simply asked the person if they liked or disliked you. By asking the person if they dislike you, you give a "no command" meta-message. They will respond with a softer, gentler tone and possibly a supportive hand on your shoulder to convey a connection. By *telling* them they *must* dislike you, you have given the meta-message of disliking you and you have instilled more resistance within them for comforting you. Even though the *"right?"* at the end of the sentence is asking for counter evidence to disliking you, the *"must"* has been reinforced over so many years by various authority figures that it has far greater emotional impact than the overall question itself. They may respond with folded arms, a scowl, and an angry or frustrated tone when the meta-message is negative or in the form of a command. How you say things or pose questions with certain tones can either increase or contradict the meta-messages.

Words themselves have an emotional impact, but it is the tone that increases the intensity of how the meta-message is delivered and received. Tone, timbre, tempo, and volume say more and may have a greater impact than the word alone. For example, if someone yells, "I love you" and has a scowl on their face, you will not typically smile and hear the words, "I love you." You will feel angry, defensive, or hurt due to the intensity of the meta-message and the tone in which it was delivered. When a false sense of self is operating and you provide a negative meta-message, the command is powerful and incredibly reinforcing to the behaviors of others and yourself. To illustrate the point thus far, try this exercise:

Say aloud, "*I hate that!*" Say it with passion and anger. Pay attention to your mood. Where do you feel it? What is your mood when you say it? Now say, "I am not at all fond of that!" Say it with the same anger and passion. What do you feel from it? What is your mood when you say it? Most likely, the anger and negative emotion is less severe with having said the latter.

One more exercise. Now say, "I hate that!" in a seductive whispering tone and at a slower tempo than you did before. Where do you feel it? What is your mood when you say it? More than likely, the feelings of intense negativity are greatly reduced. You may have even smiled when you said it.

By practicing how you say something and consciously thinking about the meta-message before the actual communication, you can change the way you see yourself and the way you are seen by others. Once you are aware of your internal identity struggle, your subconscious or conscious intentions and messages during communication, it becomes easier to change the meta-messages and improve the overall efficacy of your verbal messages. It takes practice, but becoming aware of the visceral reaction of certain words and the tone you use while talking, you can more effectively convey your positive, true identity to yourself and others.

LANGUAGE AND SELF-STATEMENTS.

Language is simply the verbal expression of your thoughts and beliefs. To further change your language, you will have to explore your thoughts and modify them to match your true self-concept. It is startling to see how proficient we are at thinking negative thoughts about ourselves thanks to our developed neuropathways.

To demonstrate, think of a list of five things you *don't* like about yourself. Now think of five things you *do* like about yourself. What was easier and which came quicker for you?

Early on, the voice or influence from others is most powerful. As an adult, there is no more powerful voice that influences the way you feel than your own. Words spoken to us by others are simply *noise* until we give that noise a meaning. When the negative and false sense of self is in operation, not only do we deliver negative messages to others, the words we hear from them are often interpreted incorrectly. Those words influence our emotions when we interpret the meaning. When the negative or false sense is strong, we interpret things in a more negative fashion. Benign comments or neutral comments may begin to be viewed as negative when you analyze the communication based on a false or negative identity. When it is easier for you to think of the negative thoughts, then it is easier for you to interpret and project negative statements as well.

By paying attention to what we tell ourselves in situations, you will be better able to regulate the way you feel and react to situations. Martin Seligman (2002) advises us to first recognize our pessimistic thoughts and then to treat them as if someone whose purpose in life is to make you miserable had spoken them. Have you ever noticed how when someone else makes a negative statement about you that you can sometimes quickly bat the negative comment away? When *you* tell yourself something negative there is no resistance; it tenaciously sticks in our consciousness and we rarely ever question or dispute the statements.

When we take our self-initiated statements and externalize them, you can rally energy for combating the negative statements and the accompanying negative emotions more readily than if they were spoken internally alone. For example, say you were to tell yourself that you *"always screw up relationships"* and that you *"will never find someone decent enough with whom to be in a relationship."* There is little to no resistance to combat this statement when you utter it to yourself. Now, imagine that a stranger walks up to you and says venomously *"you always screw up relationships."* What would be your response? Would you accept it without challenge or would you make some rebuttal or remark? More than likely, you would instinctively react protectively and say something nasty back. Or you would say something like, *"You don't know anything about me! I am a great person, I have a lot of love to give someone, and I will find someone that is right for me when the time is right."*

When someone else tells you something negative, you are more than likely to look for reasons as to why it is not true. However, when you say these negative statements to yourself, there is no one to defend or attack back because you are initiating the attack against yourself. Self-talk takes a more permanent form and is not as easy to defend against because it is internal.

Try an experiment: take one of your common negative statements like, "I feel fat," "I'm stupid," "I screw everything up," or whatever it may be. Say it aloud first as if someone else was saying it to you. Visualize someone that is venomous and spiteful making the statement to you. What visceral reaction do you have? Now say the same sentence as if you are simply telling yourself the negative statement as if it were a fact. What visceral reactions do you have? Is there a difference? Typically, thinking of someone else making the statement will allow you to do something about it and look for alternative positive countermanding statements. When you tell yourself the statements, you simply sit with the negativity and do not rally any positive reactions that effectively reduce your negative feelings.

Negative statements can be like an insidious cancer that can eat away your self-esteem and sense of self-efficacy and can become part of your core beliefs. The more you say it, the more the brain develops neuropathways to make the thought come quicker and easier, and eventually the stronger and more permanent the belief becomes.

It is important to provide you with an example at this point to see how your history and false self may be playing out in your daily interactions.

EXAMPLE:

Lea is a forty-five year old single mother. She recently divorced because of her husband's infidelity and lack of attention. She was attractive, outgoing, and was back into the dating scene. Her dating life was unsuccessful, however. After the initial interest from men, they would stop calling and avoid her calls. She was becoming frustrated and angry because she noticed that after one or two dates, the men she dated would lose interest. She wanted to discover what she was doing to cause the lack of interest in others.

We explored her home life and discovered that her father was emotionally unavailable and frequently absent from home. Much of the chores and parental responsibilities to fix things or organize family functions fell upon her. Her mother was kind and gentle but lacked the assertiveness that Lea seemed to naturally possess. Lea's mother allowed Lea to become the pseudo "father" of the house helping with household chores, preparing breakfast and packing lunches for her younger sister. Lea was expected to be the "strong one" of the family and comfort her mother and little sister during family hardships.

We explored the struggle for Lea. Her false identity was that of industry and of a paternal role. She "had to get things done," always tried to suppress her vulnerability and did not want to rely on others. Emotionally, she was driven and rarely showed anything other than her pragmatic side. Accomplishment for Lea meant receiving praise from her mother, helping her to base her identity on always taking care of others in the form of a "masculine" way. Her false identity was pragmatic, detached, and never vulnerable. Lea's true identity was revealed when she was alone. She felt vulnerable, wrote poetry, and hoped to have a less responsible role in a relationship. Her true self was more feminine and interdependent on her significant other. I asked her to give me an example of her last date and to describe the communication. Lea said the first two dates went well, but after the third date, the man never called again. Here is how she described the date and the communication:

Jason drove to Lea's house. He met her at the door with flowers. She said the flowers were nice and put them on the table without paying much attention to them or reading the attached card. Jason went to open the car door, and Lea said politely, "I can do that. I don't need anyone to open my door for me." Jason smiled and said awkwardly, "okay." They drove to a local restaurant where Lea opened the restaurant door for Jason. Jason smiled and said, "You're quite the gentleman" playfully. Lea smiled and walked past Jason and up to the hostess. "Table for two please for Lea," she said. She noticed that Jason was not saying too much when they sat at dinner so she opened the conversation by saying, "You have to try the roasted chicken. You'll love it." Jason replied, "I was thinking more of the salmon." Lea closed the menu and said, "No. You have to try the chicken. I will order it for you."

The conversation limped on for the remainder of the evening and Jason never called again. When talking with Lea, we explored her meta-message with Jason.

The meta-message that was rampant throughout the evening in verbal communication as well as behaviorally was, *"You're not capable of taking care of yourself," "You will not be able to get close to me." "Things will be on my terms and I am not going to be vulnerable."* There was no room for equality in the interaction nor was there room left for Jason to express his wishes and identity. Lea was locked into pragmatic and paternal mode leaving no room for her true self to emerge during the night.

After helping Lea *identify* her struggle, *understand* how her behavior and verbal communications reinforced her false identity, and helping her to move into the *correcting* phase, I had her do a mental exercise. I had her visualize the date again, although this time she would be on the date as her true self. She told me that if she were her true self that she would have made more comments on the kind gestures Jason made by bringing flowers and opening the car door. She said that she would have asked for more of his input throughout the evening and would have been less formal in the interaction.

Some weeks after, a co-worker asked her to dinner. Prior to the date, I had her visualize her true self and say they meta-message before beginning the date that she "will be herself and be more vulnerable." The date went well and she now has been dating the same man for over five months.

As we outlined in Lea's example, our past experiences and beliefs will sometimes be triggered in our daily lives. When you find yourself having negative beliefs about yourself or your abilities, it is important to recognize them for what they are—just beliefs not facts! Rarely are they ever facts; they are typically overreactions to situations yet we tend to accept them as facts.

Often these negative beliefs and statements are automatic so it may be helpful to write down common negative statements that you make in one day in order to help you recognize them so you can more easily understand what is triggering them. Is there a particular type of situation you are in or person that you are around when you find yourself using more negative self-statements? Pay attention to when, where, and how often you verbalize negative statements in order for you to limit the frequency you engage in automatic negative thoughts and reinforce the neuropathways. Once you have mastered your outward projection of the false identity and negative self, the task becomes maintaining the change you have begun.

Chapter Six

Breaking The Pattern of Bad Relationships

"We come to love not by finding a perfect person, but by learning to see an imperfect person perfectly."

-Anonymous-

How you interact with others and how safe you feel in any relationship will depend greatly on your early family and social interactions. If you have had a positive upbringing with a relatively healthy family, you are likely to have connected and emotionally meaningful relationships. If, on the other hand, you had an unhealthy and challenging upbringing or were exposed to an unhealthy family system, then you are likely to have frequent strife in relationships and feel lonely and unfulfilled.

What we learn early on, as far as interpersonal patterns, stays with us long after we break away from our unhealthy family systems. Aspects of our false self can be re-triggered if we engage with people that remind us of our unhealthy family system or unsafe environment. If we engage with positive people, their interaction with us can often help provide us with positive feedback for our true self. But this depends on how severe our false self is. If your false identity is strong, it will impair your interactions in relationships and prevent you from having the most fulfilled interpersonal connections even when you interact with those that have a healthy relationship history.

You may be unaware of how much your false self is impacting your relationship because you have been the super-producer persona where work tasks are your life. You may be the most productive person in the office, yet are rarely invited to any social gatherings or feel frequently shunned by those around you. Or, you may be the invisible persona always putting your needs in the background for your friends. You may be the consummate shoulder for all your friends to cry on, but when you need support, they are nowhere to be found.

Unhealthy behaviors can emerge in any relationship you engage in whether it is a friendship, intimate relationship, work or collegial relationship, or simple casual social interaction. However, intimate relationships are often the most problematic areas for triggering false identities. The more intimate the relationship, the more vulnerable we feel and the quicker our hidden issues surface and play out in the interaction.

You may have wondered why some relationships begin with bliss and quickly turn to misery. For many of us, this is due to two things: our expectations of others and others expectations for us. Initially, we begin every relationship by expecting certain behaviors from others and trying to adapt to the behaviors that the other person expects from us. Ultimately, we want connection and we begin by putting our best foot forward in the hopes that a connection will develop. As the connection begins to develop, the motivation and flexibility dissipate as a sense of predictability and security with the other person develops. When we begin to feel safe, we drop the conscious part of our behavior and the false self often emerges.

For example, when you are on a first date, you are more conscious about your physical appearance, how you speak, how you act, what "vibe" you are giving off. You effectively modify yourself to best fit the present situation and behave in such a way that will allow the other to see you in the best light. After six months or a year, you notice that you care notably less about your appearance and your behaviors toward your significant other shift to include more open defiance or criticism.

Over time in relationships, people will no longer consciously think of their behaviors, thoughts, or actions because they have become comfortable. When the relationship is new and initial interactions are unpredictable, a person may be able to engage early on with relatively healthy behaviors. When comfort and familiarity enter, the conscious mind takes a backseat and the early learning and false self take over and begin to influence behaviors. After six months or so, the seemingly perfect person begins to "unravel" to reveal the relatively flawed interior. The prince turns into the frog and the princess turns into the witch.

REPEATING THE PATTERNS:

When you have a history of early emotional injury or of an unfettered false identity, you will carry that identity and behaviors into future relationships. These behaviors, attitudes, and overall unpleasant emotional states such as anger, jealously, distrust, etc., will continue to erode at the foundations of an otherwise healthy relationship until you recognize what went wrong early on and know exactly what you want from the relationship. You will most likely begin to see a pattern in your dating habits, such as engaging in relationships with similar types of people.

When you notice that you date a particular type of person such as "the bad boy" or "the bad girl" or "the motherly type" or "the fatherly type," there are reasons you are drawn to this type of person. Identifying the "type" of person you are drawn to or have been in relationships with will help you to identity the unresolved issue and the false identity, helping to improve future relationships.

When we are young, we interact and connect more to our parents or parental figures than we do anyone else. How they chose to interact with us allows us to develop expectations and neuropathways, teaching us how to interact with those we allow into the most interpersonal sanctum of our emotions. Our early family interactions train our minds and set a behavioral framework for how we are to interact in social and interpersonal situations.

Just as each culture has certain rules, customs, and innate understanding, so too does each family. As we date and allow others to connect to us, we expect them to adapt to our style of interactions. If, for example, being passive aggressive was a pattern of behavior in your family, you may begin to utilize those similar behaviors in your relationships. They may be hidden initially, but over time become more pronounced as you become more emotionally attached to the person.

The more significant the emotional wounds in the early interactions with parents or parental figures, the unhealthier the relationships will be that develop later on. Let's say, for example, that someone has a detached mother or father figure. In their adult relationship history, we would expect that person to have a pattern of dating the "distant" woman or man, or the "bad girl" or "bad boy" or any type of person that may have difficulty attaching to others. If you are a male with a distant mother figure, then in your future relationships you may adapt the "maternal" role in your dating life as you try to lure the "distant" woman into a relationship. Unconsciously, the man will be trying to reclaim the emotional attachment that was unavailable when he was young. Initially, early in the dating relationship, the male may be overly indulgent, poetic, and hyper-romantic. However, once the man sees emotional responsiveness from the distant woman, the male may feel a sudden disinterest and quickly move onto another emotionally distant female figure.

Likewise, if you are a woman with an emotionally volatile, hostile, or distant father figure, you will be drawn to the troubled "bad boy" who will continue to devalue you and overlook your needs just as the parental figure had done. The woman will be drawn to the perceived control and machismo of the distant bad boy male, but she will experience distress, depression, and overall misery as she feels the continued rejection from this distant and emotionally unavailable male. Even if the woman decided to pursue the "nice guy" type, she may find herself dissatisfied, flirting with the "bad boy" type, pushing the nice guy away, or creating frequent arguments as she struggles with her false identity and the pain with early rejection and emotions from the distant male parent.

Like having an itch that you never can fully scratch, many people try to offset past hurt and emotional pain by pursuing a future with someone else. They may be chasing relationship after relationship only to feel some further rejection or disappointment they experienced early in life because they are chasing past hurt rather than future and present happiness. By chasing the ghost of the past when starting relationships, they never really see the actual person in front of them and this "relationship blindness" impairs any healthy interaction that may occur without the experience of the past hurt.

When past hurt has occurred in early family interaction, unconsciously, people that have been hurt will play out their internalized and hidden feelings of rejection, anger, and abandonment when they pursue relationships in the adult years. Without addressing the hurt and seeing the false self and how it is playing out in relationship dynamics, people repeat the pattern of rejection. People who hold onto the past hurt continue to feel unsafe in relationships and believe they will be ultimately rejected. Or they may preemptively reject the person they want in the relationship before they can be rejected themselves. The person that has the past hurt wants to stop the pain from the past by pursuing relationship after relationship. Often people are too afraid to become emotionally connected to someone because they feel that they cannot endure the emotional pain again.

By rejecting the person they love now before the relationship and attachment occurs, they may be not only trying to avoid pain but can sometimes be unconsciously trying to "get even" with the past attachment figures that initially created the false identity. The person may be hypercritical of partners and oftentimes openly domestically violent in some extreme cases when they are trying to get even with past hurt.

PAST HURT EQUALS FUTURE REJECTION

If you have emotionally distant parental figure, you may begin to treat your lover or significant other in the same capacity because you have the pain of feeling loneliness and abandonment already operating within you.

The thought of allowing someone closer into your heart brings back that sense of being vulnerable. If that person abandons you, the pain of that loss only compounds with early abandonment. The pain becomes unbearable. The thought of having to endure that pain will raise the wall and rather than allowing someone too close, you will say hurtful things or engage in defense mechanisms to hold your significant other at arm's length to protect yourself. Without realizing it, holding someone at arm's length only ensures that self-fulfilling prophecy of abandonment because you push them away and block their attempts at getting close and developing healthy emotional connections with you. After a while, your significant other feels dejected and abandoned by your blocked efforts and they move on, now bearing scars of their own based on your rejection of them.

If one of your parents was emotionally distant, it leaves a certain sense of rejection and a fear of abandonment within you. Because we allow only those we love into our innermost emotional realms, the fear of abandonment is carried over into relationships because only significant others and parental figures occupy the similar emotional space within us. Hence, we will sometimes seek out a partner with similar emotionally distant attributes in an attempt to reclaim the perceived lost love from a parent. Depending on the parental relationship, we will either sacrifice much of who we are to gain the emotional attachment from a significant other or we will opt to reject them before they are allowed to become too emotionally close to us. Let's give an example of Deirdre to highlight this in more detail.

EXAMPLE:

Deirdre was a thirty-six year old single attorney. She was attractive and highly accomplished as the top attorney for her firm. Her childhood was great up until the age of eight. When she was eight, her mother suddenly left her and her five-year old brother at her grandmother's doorstep. Her mother said nothing; she simply left, and was never seen again. It was later discovered that her mother had returned to her native country of Colombia because she felt that she was not ready for motherhood. Deirdre had no idea why her mother had gone and became depressed and withdrawn as a child. Her grandmother who then raised her was ill and required quite of bit of daily care. Deirdre was soon doing cooking and cleaning for her younger brother and her grandmother. Deirdre would get her brother ready for school and after school would prepare dinner, essentially functioning as the head of the household. She excelled in school and sports never having any downtime and always accomplishing goal after goal.

As an adult, she moved from one place to another never feeling settled. Her dating life was short-lived and she dated men that always needed someone to care for them in some way. She was always in the caregiver role with whomever she became romantically involved. At one time, she began to date an emotionally healthy man, but soon after, became highly critical and emotionally more distant. She tried to buy him things and take care of him. He politely rejected the unwanted and excessive care she forced upon him. She became more anxious and distracted, seeing his independent side and that she was not able to take care of him as she had everyone else. Small arguments became nasty fights as the relationship continued. She would attack and scold him over simple things. Eventually, after one bitter diatribe she unleashed, he left without saying a word. The next day, Deidre moved and took another job and never looked back.

Deidre began to get close and had a difficult time managing the fear of rejection. Because she had only felt connection or needed when she was the caregiver, she was not able to endure the uncertainty of being in a balanced and healthy relationship. She needed to feel that she was in control and that the men needed her. She had faced a tremendous emotional blow early on in her life when her mother left, so when she was not able to control the relationship, she felt lost and uncertain. Rather than wait for the rejection to occur, Deidre pushed and scolded to unconsciously hasten the dissolution of the relationship because not having the control was frightening and uncertain for her. Her fear blinded her to the potential of the relationship and she essentially rejected him before he had the opportunity to reject her. When he left, she felt vindicated and fell back into her survival mode to protect herself again. Even though she cared more deeply for the man she criticized the most, her past hurt guaranteed future rejection of those with whom she felt the most emotionally vulnerable.

WHY WE HURT THE ONES WE LOVE

The more we love someone, the less we utilize our thinking. When we are comfortable, we allow some of our mind to relax and allow more of our emotional parts to be expressed. If there is emotional pain, frustration, and anger reserved from early learning, our comfort with those we love allows the negative emotions to surface unchecked by our logic and reasoning.

If we have not explored our past and recognized our false identity, we will continue to replay rejection and try unconsciously to keep people at a distance emotionally. The wall we put up between ourselves and those we love is not only to protect us, but it is a way for us to "get even" with those that have hurt us in the past. Our unconscious mind has the meta-message of *"don't let anyone too close"* or *"I don't want to be like my parents…"* or *"I am pissed off at my father for never being around,"* or whatever message that reflects your past. This message is stored and operates with greater ease the more comfortable we get with someone and the more we begin to develop an attachment to that person.

The man that loves his wife yet remains within the grips of a false persona from past hurts may begin to drink, say hurtful things, or do hurtful things to push her away. The woman that loves her man may reject him sexually or make herself too busy for those times where emotional connection can happen. We hurt those we love not because we are sadistic by nature; we hurt the ones we love because those we love occupy the closest form of interpersonal connection. Managing that connection is difficult due to our previous learning and past experience of hurt and rejection.

GOOD RELATIONSHIPS TURNED BAD

Whether you are miserable or happy in a relationship is a decision that you make consciously and unconsciously. Initially, it is a conscious decision that later becomes an unconscious decision once the comfort and safety is developed in the relationship. At the beginning of a relationship, you are consciously deciding if you like the person, if he/she can sustain your interest, if you enjoy spending time with that person, etc. The emotional tie is not there so your conscious mind is free to make decisions to continue the relationship or not.

After interacting with a person for a while, an emotional bond develops and comfort and familiarity are established. Together, an emotional tie has been developed to where you have adopted some behaviors inherent to the other person and the other person has adopted some of your own behaviors and personality quirks. When this emotional tie is allowed to develop, fear can also arise, as there is no longer the ability to walk away without some emotional consequence. When you reach the point of no return where you can no longer walk away without emotional pain, you will resort to unconscious defense mechanisms to protect yourself when the false identity is in operation.

You may resort to stonewalling or acting emotionally distant to keep the other person emotionally distant as well. Or, you may do passive-aggressive things to create arguments that elicit anger so that you can hide your true emotions behind the wall of anger. Some examples of this may include leaving dishes in the sink day after day when you know it will irritate your significant other or intentionally not making phone calls when you are aware that not calling will make your significant other worry.

Have you ever wondered why someone close to you angers you so much? Many of us are far less annoyed by total strangers than we are by those close to us. Anger is frequently found in relationships because we have learned that it is a tool of protection. Especially for men, anger is the only emotion they are allowed to express, so men utilize anger in many relationships as a way to contain vulnerable feelings.

Anger serves an adaptive, albeit unhealthy function in relationships. When you are angry, you feel no other emotions. Anger is an effective emotional anesthetic. When you are feeling vulnerable or afraid, anger is typically the next step as we unconsciously seek out ways to stop the emotional discomfort. Anger is a simple defense mechanism albeit one with destructive results for relationships. We hurt the ones we love simply because we love them and they occupy a space of emotional vulnerability with us.

How frequently you hurt others you love emotionally or employ unhealthy defense mechanisms depends on your past experiences and your future expectations. If you expect to be hurt in a relationship or interaction, your defense mechanisms will arise and linger until you feel safe. If you expect to be loved and are willing to give your all in the relationship, the defense mechanisms will not be triggered and you will be able to ride out a rough patch without anger and resorting to destructive behaviors.

How the relationship turns out depends on how it begins. Many relationships begin on a faulty premise that only serves to reinforce the negative, false sense of self. People say, "*I have been hurt before in the past, and I am not going to let anyone do that to me again!*" Beginning a relationship—or any life endeavor for that matter—based on what you *do not want* only allows you to inadvertently live life by fear. Fear and what you don't want then becomes your compass by which you navigate your life.

HIDDEN AGENDAS: DAMAGING THE RELATIONSHIP

When you operate with negative self-directives such as, "I will not do that again!" you then set your eyes for focusing on failure alone. The positive is completely missed because you are unconsciously looking for failure and what you do not want. If I say, "Do not think of a beautiful, calm ocean and sunset," what do you do? Obviously, you think about a sunset because I said don't think of a sunset.

If you have a negative sense of self-operating within you, you may be replaying and reinforcing your negative self-beliefs daily without even knowing it. You may be looking for what you don't want without even knowing it. If you have been exposed to an unhealthy family system where the needs of others always came first, you will feel a strange familiarity with a particular person that represents some aspect of that past behavior. Going back to the example of Melissa in Chapter One, she had a domineering brother and an emotionally detached father. Melissa had to navigate that family system for years trying not to upset her father or brother. If she meets a domineering male, like her brother, or an apathetic male, like her father, she may feel a certain and peculiar attraction to them because those were the two closest males to her growing up. Her years of familiarity and expertise at making both her father and brother happy will translate into her being particularly adept at initiating and sustaining unhealthy relationships with men that are similar to either her brother and/or father.

Even if Melissa were to encounter men with traits similar to her brother or father but not as severe, her behavior and actions may reinforce and intensify the traits of domineering or apathy. Melissa may always be attentive, never asking for anything or refusing the male opportunities to reciprocate. She may withdraw from time to time or do passive aggressive behaviors that will anger the domineering male only then to be completely attentive. By being attentive after angering someone, Melissa would have conditioned or trained the male on how to get his emotional needs met. Being angry equals emotional connection.

Many people replay these dynamics in relationships without even realizing it. As we mentioned early in Chapter Four, what you say may be changing the behaviors in your partner and friends. Since most relationships are emotionally based, if your emotions are a bit off, then you can expect your relationship to feel a bit off as well. In whatever way you feel about yourself, you will project that ideal into the relationship and expect the other to respond to how you see yourself and how others in the past have interacted with you. This is known as *projective identification*. We all do this to some degree in relationships, but some do this more than others do. How devastating this projective dynamic is depends on how serious our past was and what our goals for the future are.

Ultimately, as evidenced by Melissa, we try to replay the early life family dynamic that helped to shape and define us, as well as our social interaction. Like Melissa, when we have a false identity operating within, we will re-engage in interpersonal patterns that are familiar to us. We replay this dynamic not because we like the misery, but because we want to change the dynamic itself and ultimately change our own self-image. However, by replaying the dynamic with significant others in our adult life, we only serve to reinforce the same behaviors that led us astray because we keep triggering the old behavioral patterns and interactions that we established as a child. As I said earlier, you cannot unlearn how to ride a bicycle; you cannot unlearn how to be proficient at unhealthy relationship but, like learning how to ride a four-wheeler, you can learn to become proficient at healthy relationships.

IMPROVING YOUR RELATIONSHIPS.

With all relationships and families alike, balance is the primary goal. Even in unhealthy relationships and families, the family strives toward a harmony by having one person make up for the deficits of the other. Whoever holds the most emotional reservoir or is more persistent in asserting needs in the relationship will change the behavior of the other in the relationship. When one person pushes forward with their needs, the other person will fall back to compensate for the push to regain balance in the relationship. The problem is that some push too far while others give too much and relationships become unhealthy for the individual while balanced for the relationship unit.

As we discussed in the stages of change, the most important component of stopping the unhealthy relationship is first by identification. When you explore your struggle and identify it clearly, you can then identity your part in trying to balance out the unhealthy family system. By exploring the role of your primary care givers, such as your parents, you can see where they were lacking or what they were unconsciously asking you to do such as *"emotionally contain me"* or *"take care of the household because I am unable to do so."* By exploring your responses and your interactions during times of crisis, you can see your contributions to sustaining the family system. You can also see how you may be continuing this same behavioral intervention in your current relationships.

It is a wise idea to go back and look at your past relationships. Explore the similarities in the relationships and why the relationships failed. Even if the failure was not your fault, explore your contributions to the relationship. Use the spaces below to look at your past patterns of interaction in relationships and family interaction.

1. **Some of the traits I have in common with people I have dated are:**

   a._____

   b._____

   c._____

2. **When I look back, I can see where I did too much of or not enough of:**

   a._____

   b._____

   c._____

3. **Looking back at my early family interaction, my role to find balance or make things right was to:**

   a._____

   b._____

   c._____

4. **When I am initially attracted to someone, I notice first:**

   a._____

   b._____

   c._____

There is such a thing as a perfect relationship if your perfect relationship takes into account the imperfection of others and the occasional head-butting that occurs in every relationship and interaction. The perfection lies not in the fairy-tale ideal of a flawless relationship, but in how you express yourself, how you listen to the wishes and concerns of your significant other, and how you both focus on a solution instead of the problem when a disagreement arises. Taking your past behavioral patterns into account, how your past hurt may influence your self-expression and give rise to defense mechanisms, and setting clear goals for what you want and need out of a relationship is the best way to reinforce your true self.

With your expectations of others or your significant other, be sure that what you need from the relationship or the person is not simply the very thing that was lacking in your family interaction. Setting a goal to make up for something that has already been done will leave the person you expect to undo the damage feeling overwhelmed and isolated. When you set your goals for the relationship, keep in mind balance—balance for what you need and what you can give. Many people look for "the other half" of themselves in a lover. By looking for the other half, you have already set off empty and when you start the search empty, you will end up more empty and depleted. You need to start off "whole" and find someone that enhances what you have rather than brings something for which you are searching. Start off positive, look for the positive, and you will find and receive positive. Using positive communication is the easiest and quickest way to improve relationships and interactions.

COMMUNICATION IN RELATIONSHIPS.

There are basic techniques that can assist you in facilitating your communication to reinforce your true self and for your communication to reinforce the true self in your significant other. The first is to understand that we all communicate differently, especially men and women.

It's no secret that women and men have different communication styles. There is some evidence that supports the fact that men and women use their brains differently when it comes to communication. Most notably, women use more of the emotional centers of the brain when communicating. It may be cultural rather than genetic but when men communicate with men, they are direct and short. A subtle grunt, a quick head nod, or firm knuckle-to-knuckle greeting. When women communicate with women, the emotional understanding is obvious by the facial expression, the sympathetic nod or touch on the shoulder, and the kind words of support offered.

The pragmatic or "logic" approach to communication by men may lead them astray in arguments because arguments are primarily emotional in nature not logical in nature. When a disagreement starts, men may want to solve the problem even before they clearly understand what the problem is. By overlooking the emotional component to the argument, the emotional unrest will only heighten and make a small issue become a big argument. Here are the four steps to minimize contention in conversations:

1. Listen to the problem completely. Take notes if necessary but allow your significant other to finish his/her thoughts and feelings about the situation. Look for the emotions behind the situation. For example, if he/she says *"I am hurt by the fact that you forgot my birthday."* Rather than go into explanations immediately, acknowledge the fact that he/she is experiencing hurt feelings and give him/her time to express their feelings uninterrupted. Once he/she has expressed herself, ask for clarification to ensure you understood the issue.

2. Clarify the problem and repeat back. Repeat back what you understood the issue to be. For example, you might say, *"I understand that you are hurt by the fact that I forgot your birthday. Is that right?"* Once you understand the issue, being compassionate for the way he/she feels and sees things leads to his/her feeling safe and allows for the defensive guard to fall away.

3. Be supportive and acknowledge their side of the issue. Even if you felt you had good reason for the issue, wait until you hear his/her side out completely. You will have a chance to explain your side, but it is absolutely necessary to allow him/her to discuss their side. Be patient and acknowledge your side of the argument or what your take was on what contributed to the argument. For example, say, *"I'm sorry for missing your birthday. I understand how that could have hurt your feelings."* Ask for clarification to ensure that you understood her/his side completely. Once all the issues are on the table, it is then time to move to the problem side.

4. Problem solving. After the issue has been clarified, together ask one another for solutions to rectify the situation. Initiate the problem-solving phase by something like, *"It was not my intention at all to hurt your feelings. I am sorry if what I said hurt your feelings. Is there any way I can make up for hurting your feelings? This is what I feel I can do to make up for...what do you think?"*

Communication is essential for every relationship to be successful. Each person will need to listen to the partner's needs and be able to express his/her own needs in the relationship to their partner. Oftentimes, previous hurt or false identities, like the invisible persona, diminish the ability for people to communicate effectively. For effective communication, you need to be able to identify your strengths and to feel that what you offer or what your needs are will be important to the relationship. Each person needs to feel and be aware of the value they bring to the relationship in order for communication to be successful and effective. Take the time now to identify your strengths that you bring to the relationship. When you are aware of your strengths, you can more freely express your needs.

1. **The positive traits I bring to any relationship are:**

    a._____

    b._____

    c._____

    d._____

    e._____

    f._____

No matter how good your communication style is, there can be a breakdown in communication. Arguments can impair communication from time to time. Communication can go wrong quickly when anger builds and sometimes hurt can last long after the argument has subsided.

Arguments and relationship problems often highlight the negative or the problematic behaviors. As mentioned earlier, one negative comment can offset twenty positive comments, so when arguments or communication only involves the negative, it can quickly destroy the positive sense of self. By knowing your positive traits and the positive things you bring to the relationship, you can weigh the negative statements for validity. When in an argument, be sure to remind yourself of the positive things and ask your partner for some of the positives as well. Do not allow the negatives to slowly chip away your positive sense of self.

Maintaining positive communication and a positive sense of self involves you issuing positives to your significant others. By initially knowing what you want out of a relationship and what you like about your partner/significant other will help you see the positive things with more clarity. Arguments focus on negatives but daily interaction should focus on the positives.

Everyone should make time for positive statements. When your significant other looks good, cooks well, or does something kind and spontaneous, comment on what you observe. Say, "You look great?" or "that was so thoughtful of you," or "that means so much to me that you did that." Positive interactions and statements are expected but rarely do we comment on it. By shifting the focus onto the positives and taking time to highlight the positive interactions you begin to build up an emotional reservoir of positive things to counteract the negatives that the occasional argument will take away.

2. **What I like most about my partner/significant other is:**

    a._____

    b._____

    c._____

    d._____

    e._____

    f._____

Even if an argument or disagreement begins, start off with the positive in mind. By beginning with the positive, you lessen the impact and hurtful nature of the discussion. If you have a concern and would like to discuss it with your significant other, start with the final goal in mind. Begin the opening statement with a positive remark, and focus on the emotion you feel.

For example, begin the conversation by saying, "You have been wonderful at the past dinner parties we have attended. At this one, I felt hurt and humiliated by some things you said. Could we talk about it for a few moments?" This is much better at lowering the guard and beginning a conversation with rectifying in mind rather than anger. If you say, "you were a complete jerk tonight!" you could see how going on the offensive would bring up a wall and nothing will be accomplished other than mudslinging and more hurt.

If your goal is to express your hurt and find ways to prevent it from happening again, then you will tend to choose more positive words and more constructive phrases when beginning the communication. Keep in mind that what you give out in communication, you will receive in return. Give out anger, you receive anger; give out positive and openness and you receive positive and openness.

If you give out positive messages on finding a solution together when you have disagreements, you will most likely receive the same from your significant other. Remember that if you would like the person to do something or stop doing something, the best way to achieve this goal is by telling them what they did in the past that you enjoyed or would like them to do more. People don't change permanently by punishment or punitive phrases. We change by praise. Praise feels good to receive and so being human, we naturally gravitate toward the pursuit of pleasurable things. Reinforce positive behaviors and statements and you will see more of them from your significant other.

Tell your significant others about their successes in the past at helping you to feel happy with them, and you have helped them find a way to continue to make you happy in the future.

BE SPONTANEOUS AND CREATIVE

Many in relationships allow routine and outside roles such as jobs and/or parental responsibilities to drain all passion and spontaneity form the relationship. For example, schedule at least one night a week to go out to dinner, a movie, or a walk. Not with the kids, Uncle Johnny, or the neighbors—just the two of you. Go to your favorite restaurant, the one you went to on your first date, or the one that has positive memories. Make it a special night, get dressed up, buy some flowers for your partner, or get a card, write a poem, or whatever it is that will show your affection. It will also show that you are willing to take the extra step to show them that you still love them and enjoy being with them. Take turns being spontaneous. For two weeks, have it be your responsibility to come up with the spontaneous night, and the following two weeks as their responsibility to balance interests and responsibility.

Be creative in finding ways to show your significant other that you care. Put notes on their side of the mirror in the bathroom so they awaken to a nice message. Put a cute IOU in their coat pocket or purse before work, anything simple that lets them know they are in your thoughts. It makes a big difference in saying what may not be said as much in your relationship—that you love them.

Relationships can be rewarding, enrich your life experience, and allow you to feel more connected to people. It takes work to foster healthy relationships and for you to give and receive the most that a relationship has to offer. Once you have dealt with issues that may interfere with your relationships and/or your interpersonal interactions, the potential for connectedness and meaningful relationships with family, friends, and loved ones is likely to improve. All healthy relationships begin with each person being aware of his/her issues as well as their strengths. Personal growth is often the forerunner to a healthy relationship. We will now discuss the various stages of growth and changes that you are likely to progress through on your way to a more fulfilled life.

Chapter Seven

Beginning Phases for Change & Growth

"People handle their fear of change in different ways, but the fear is inescapable if they are in fact to change."

-M Scott Peck, MD-

Change does not happen in one fell swoop; nor is it typically something that happens automatically. Change is something that requires work and patience. It evolves one day at a time and with conscious effort. Growth may be slow initially and there may be a few hurdles or setbacks that will happen along the way, but change will occur if you are patient and persistent.

When you first begin the steps towards change, it may seem somewhat discouraging when progress and change does not appear to happen fast enough. Some can give up easily or get frustrated with themselves when they find themselves repeating past destructive behaviors or finding that they have had a few setbacks. With any change or progress, there will always be some setbacks or challenges along the way that, eventually, you will find are not insurmountable. You will find that change is a process, a fluid and dynamic process, which can bend and mold with life events. With time and patience, progress is inevitable if you have the proper motivation for change and a solidified plan for what change looks like for you.

When you are taking steps towards changing yourself, your behaviors, and ultimately your future, keep in mind that it took many years to learn unhealthy behaviors. It is natural that it should take awhile to develop and learn new healthy behaviors that are more conducive to the growth of the true self and a positive future.

It is a good idea to have a realistic view on the process of change and to be aware of the phases of growth that you will travel through towards lasting change in your life. Initially, change can bring about discomfort and be difficult to accept, but it becomes easier with time and effort. Like moving a freight train, change and growth may initially seem overwhelming with the effort, but once the momentum is up, there is little that can stop the progress towards a healthier and happier life.

There are various stages of growth for initiating change but, for our purposes, we will focus on three primary phases for changing your struggles and beginning your new path toward your true self. These three phases are the Identification phase, the Understanding & Correcting phase, and the Maintenance phase.

STAGE I

The first phase is the **identification** phase. In order for change and growth to happen, you must first identify the struggle itself. The purpose of chapters one through four was to discuss the concept of the struggle and provide you with the means to recognize and conceptualize the internal struggle that you may be facing.

The identification phase is typically the most difficult to begin because it requires that you look at painful issues of the past and your own contributions to your difficulties. It is the first phase when you step from the survival mode into a more vulnerable and self-aware stage where you are able to examine your situation and yourself. The identification phase is where insight occurs, where your eyes are finally open to your life and potential, but a clear goal or direction has not yet been formed. Initially, this phase is the most tenuous and uncertain because you are more self-aware and more vulnerable but do not yet have a concrete plan of change. It often is the phase where emotional unrest or uncertainty can occur because you are starting to look at your life without the protection of a false persona.

The identification phase is difficult for many people due to the unpleasant emotions that can occur with it such as depression, anxiety, and fear. In fact, this phase is where many people often are, without realizing it, when depression first starts to impact their life. This is where the struggle of the false self and true self meet at the crossroads, and uncertainty about what direction to proceed with their life occurs.

The temporary emotional discomfort that people begin to feel when they are more aware of their true self is one of the greatest obstacles for most individuals for progressing forward and achieving long-term growth. They have spent most of their lives trying not to feel or be aware of the emotional pain deep inside. They have lived a life of distraction and when they stop the survival mode and allow the past to catch up, it can be a bit overwhelming.

Sometimes, it is not just the fear of the past that causes some emotional discomfort, but may include having to give up what was familiar to them or what allowed them to feel connected to people in the past. Even for a false self, there are some positive reinforcements that make it difficult to let the past behaviors go entirely. Letting go of the behaviors that have kept them safe can include a sense of loss, detachment, and even grief.

For example, with alcohol addiction, people may initially feel grief and loss when they become aware of their drinking problems. Stopping drinking means letting go of all the behaviors associated with drinking. They realize that they have to stop going to their favorite bar, change their familiar routine of visiting their favorite liquor store or winery after work, or they have to stay away from alcoholic friends with whom they shared the addiction and spent a large portion of their time. They may feel a sense of loss at having to change the regular routines that they often planned their whole life around because of the addiction that was controlling them. Initially, the grief occurs because they have engaged in the behaviors for a long time and now they are letting go of them, but soon, they develop new and healthier routines and they pass through the grief and the initial difficulty associated with change.

The identification phase is the most crucial phase for change because it is where people can either commit to growth and make a difference in their lives or fall back into old patterns of unhealthy behaviors if they cannot see the long-term benefits of change. When people struggle with the identification phase, they may choose to ignore the struggle or distract themselves in some way to keep from having to do anything about it. Some fall back into past patterns and never more forward because fear has blinded them to the rewards of a happier and more fulfilled life. Others are able to move past the emotional difficulties of the identification phase and look more closely at their life. They can see what their future will entail if they live life on their terms and more in line with their true self.

Identifying and accepting the struggle takes courage and faith in your own strengths to move beyond the identification phase and make lasting changes. It takes strength to admit that there are aspects of your life that are contributing to and sustaining your own destructive patterns and struggles. Identification is the important first step towards growth but not the only phase for change.

Once you have identified that you have a struggle and have developed an understanding of how it came into existence and the behaviors that support it, then you will be better able to move into the next phase of growth and change.

STAGE II

The second phase of growth and change is the **understanding and correcting** phase. Once you have identified that you are in a struggle where depression and strife exist in your life, the next phase it to understand how that struggle plays out and to take steps towards making positive changes.

The understanding and correcting phase is a more in-depth exploration of your struggle beyond just identifying that a struggle exists. This phase moves beyond a general concept of how a false self and the true self contribute to depression and the strife within you. This phase of change allows you to recognize specific patterns in your life that fuel the struggle and is the phase where you begin to look clearly at a plan for how you can change your future. You reach the understanding and correcting phase when you have explored the negative messages that you have internalized and are aware of when these negative messages are triggered in social and interpersonal interactions and you commit to making changes in your life.

The exercise at the end of Chapter Four was the first part of the understanding and correcting phase where it allowed you to concretely write out the struggle you are facing and highlight both the false self and the true self that are in opposition within you. In other previous chapters, we discussed how the meta-messages delivered in your speech, your body language and in your personal beliefs are playing into maintaining your false identity in social interactions and are part of this phase.

This phase allows you to pull everything together to give you a clear picture of your struggle, your contributing behaviors to the struggle, and it allows you to develop a plan for correcting the behaviors and ending the struggle.

The understanding and correcting phase tends to be somewhat easier to progress and follow through than the identification phase because it allows you to be more proactive with approaches to changes. With identification, you experience friction as you struggle with past familiarity and uncertain future goals. However, with the understanding and correcting phase of growth, you have committed to the process of change and have stepped into more proactive approaches to growth so there is more inertia and less friction. You feel more in control of the process of change. You actively explore specific behaviors and actions from the past and plan corrective behaviors for the future.

This is a phase where you can more clearly see the patterns of the false identity that are playing out in your personal, occupational, and romantic life. It is the phase when your eyes are open to the effects of the false self and you start to see more clearly the potential for your life and for your true self.

With the understanding and correcting phase, a person typically has more energy, improved mood, and focuses on personal goals. We have all been in the understanding and correcting phase even if we were not aware of it. To give you an example, think of a fairly significant relationship that you have been in that ended. At first, you were depressed and thought about the fears of being alone. After a while, you began to see the destructive side of the relationship and what the relationship, and your sacrifices, took from you. You began to see a brighter future for yourself and likely started seeking out new social engagements, started to take yoga classes or exercised more, or felt a general increase in energy and vitality. You felt more in control of your life at this phase.

The understanding and correcting phase is probably the easiest to progress through due to the positive momentum that change can bring about initially. However, to sustain growth at this phase, there must be a long-term plan in effect. Like riding a wave, the understanding and correcting phase brings a surge of energy and vitality as you start a new life so to speak, but eventually the newness wears off and regression can occur if you do not have a plan in place to track your progress.

Without a plan and monitoring that plan, growth stops and you can repeat your destructive patterns of the past when the newness of change wears off and the old familiar neuropathways kick in to guide your behaviors. A very specific and vivid picture of the final goal for you should be developed in this stage of growth and change.

In order to accomplish this, visualize a mental photograph of one scenario that would represent what the final outcome of growth would look like to you. If you would like to be a better parent, imagine a mental photograph of yourself in that role where you are doing everything that would represent what being a good parent means to you. It could be something like imagining a birthday party where all the kids are having fun, a school function where you are being supportive, or where you are hiking with your child who has a look of amazement and wonder on his/her face. Whatever the role or changes you wish to see, see them in your mind as clearly as if you were staring at a real photograph. You will want to create a static photograph with as much detail as possible.

Once you have one main mental picture in your mind, you will want to visualize it as much as possible. Put reminders around the house to think of the picture that represents your goal. By bringing your future expectations into clear mental awareness in the present moment, you start to subtly shift your thoughts, behaviors, and feelings to match up with the mental image. You effectively begin to redefine your present and your future simultaneously because your positive image is serving as a polestar by which you are now navigating your life. Without the end in sight, the beginning of change never really happens. The more clearly you see the visual representation of your goal, the easier it is to accomplish, especially if you put small markers of performance in as well.

With small markers of performance, all you have to do is to think about what change looks like for you for that day. You will want to make small goals or do small tasks that represent some aspect of the goal. For example, say that you want to be a better parent and you have an image of seeing your child happy and interactive at a birthday party. When you remind yourself of that mental image each day, also think of what you might do today that would allow you to feel that you are on the right track for your goal. You will want to break the future goals into small daily goals like seeing your child happy today, or receiving a "thank you" or hug from them. Think about what you can do today that would be representative of your future self or goal. You may think of reading a bedtime story to your child or playing a game where you see your child happy and interactive. The goals initially do not have to be big, and actually should not be big, but rather manageable and even subtle goals that are attainable. By having small and attainable goals each day, they become cumulative over time until the mental image you hold in your mind becomes clearer and more real. Having small goals allows your overall goals to be achieved easier and without drastic upheaval in daily routines.

When you are able to see the change clearly with manageable steps and markers to accomplishing those goals, you will see change actually begin to unfold in various aspects of your life. Let me give you an example of how to make some goals for change, how they may look for you, and to cover some of the concepts we have examined thus far:

Rebecca has been depressed for four years, off and on. She is thirty-four years old, has two children, has a good job, a supportive husband, and has been married for six years now. One day, she felt that depression lingered longer than it ever had in the past. She sought out therapy.

In therapy, she stated that she wants to "become happy again." After exploring her life, I could find no direct cause of her sadness, no unfaithful husband, no sick child, no domineering boss—nothing that would provide a direct link to her current state of sadness. However, there were some neglect issues early on in her life that left her feeling sad and oftentimes alone as a child. We discussed the false self that may have developed with her childhood experiences. She recognized her struggle and understood how she may at times emotionally pull herself back with her family. We worked on her understanding her struggles to take some steps towards change. However, some of her depression still remained. So I asked her what that would her life look like if she were "happy again," how would she know when she was happy, and what could she do to be at least, "less sad."

She stated that she did not know what her life would look like or what would be different in her life, but it would simply "feel better." She stated that she would feel less tired, less worthless, less depressed. I gave her a scenario. I said, "Pretend that I have a magic wand and I could magically 'make you happy' again. I wave this wand tonight while you are sleeping, although you do not know that I have done this. You wake up in the morning after this magic spell has been cast. What be the first thing that would give you an indication that things had changed for you? What would be the first thing you would say as you stand in front of the bathroom mirror looking at yourself? How would your day be different than it is now? What would you do on that day that was different? How would you interact with family and friends differently? How would you walk, talk, stand, and present yourself?" After I had asked this, she looked at me and said simply, "I would like the person I saw in the mirror." "That is an excellent first step," I said. "Now tell me what specific things you would like about yourself." She replied, "I would like my smile, the way I look. I would talk with more confidence. I would be happier when my husband came home and when my kids were around. I would probably make him dinner and spend more time with my kids before their bedtime." "Excellent," I said. "If all those things happened and you interacted with your husband and kids the way you would like to, how would they respond to you?" She said, "They would be more loving and happier." I asked, "How would that feel for you if they interacted with you and were happier?" "I would be happier," she replied.

Rebecca's response is typical in that when there is not a concrete goal set in place, or when we do not know what change would look like for us, we feel stagnant, lost, and overwhelmed. By clearly visualizing a goal for what change looks like for you and setting small steps and markers for what you can do each day, no matter how small, change will happen.

The goal, as in the case of Rebecca, does not have to be a massive, life-altering goal to improve your mood or your view of happiness. Starting with changing the way you see yourself and making small behavioral changes, like making dinner or reading a bedtime story to your children, go a long way toward achieving your goal. Making even small daily goals can lead to the larger picture of change. Having a clear picture for what the goal looks like for your life is important to maintain that change and to create motivation.

When we can create a picture of what the final goal would look like for us and how we would interact differently if the goals were accomplished, we bring the future changes into the present moment and more into our control. By asking yourself how your life now would be different today if the final changes had happened overnight, you can break the feelings of helplessness and hopelessness that often stifle growth.

By creating a mental image for your true self by seeing positive outcomes, you will shift your perspective to one of success rather than failure. You feel more empowered and are more likely to start and continue towards growth rather than fall back into familiar and unhealthy patterns. By focusing on positive outcomes and a positive future, you lessen anxiety, depression, and the fear of change.

With daily visualizations of a mental photograph and awareness of your subtle body and verbal languages, you will slowly begin to align your behaviors with those future expectations. The more often you hold this image in mind, the quicker and more readily your neuropathways will adopt to believing these changes and helping you to actually become the changes you think about.

With a plan in place after you have achieved identification and understanding, change is more likely to continue. There can be some challenges with continued growth after we start change, even when change starts to become familiar. This takes us into the maintenance phase.

STAGE III

The third and final phase is the **maintenance** phase. This is the phase of maintaining lasting change and progress. After you identify your struggle, understand how it came into being and how it's negatively impacting you from discovering your true self, it's time for maintaining the growth you have made along the way.

However, the maintenance stage is the second most challenging phase of growth because after the surge of energy that comes from the understanding and correcting phase, there is a drop in motivation as familiarity takes away the energy and excitement of trying new endeavors. This phase requires a great deal of effort to keep the forward momentum because the false self and old familiar behaviors of the past begin to tug at you for attention as the "newness" energy of the understanding and correcting phase fades.

This maintenance phase is the phase that most people never tell you about when they talk about having goals. They rarely, if ever, provide you techniques for how to follow through with a goal or change once you have achieved the goal. There is almost no goal that does not require motivation or maintenance. Getting a house requires fixing and painting with age; marriage requires effort to remain strong; making money requires careful spending and planning so you don't spend every dime. Most every goal, in some way, requires maintenance; yet so often it is the one aspect that is overlooked.

For example, we are told, "Save money for a rainy day"; "have kids and get married"; "or "work out and be healthier." Since we were children, we have been given thousands upon thousands of goals that we need to accomplish. However, no one tells you what to do once you get the goals underway or achieve them. How do you keep a good marriage once you get married or how do you parent once you have kids? We are told, "Work out and change your diet." How do you stay motivated for years on an exercise program once you learn the latest techniques or are no longer overweight? We are told, "Save your money for a rainy day," but how do you initially save that money and what do you spend money on when the rainy day comes? When it comes to change, we are only taught partial techniques for change. By learning techniques from the maintenance phase, change is far easier to sustain.

The maintenance phase, like the initial identification phase, will require frequent monitoring and positive reinforcement for you to have continued motivation to achieve your goals. With the maintenance phase, you will have to take steps to monitor progress and continue with things that motivate you to stay on track and endure the monotony once the comfort sets in and the newness of change wears off.

With continued small goals and reminders for why you are making the change, the motivation will come easier and stay longer than without frequent small reminders or rewards. The goal is to have things that keep us motivated and offer small bits of progress often enough to where we are able to push through the stagnant familiarization of behaviors until the healthy become so automatic that you simply engage in them without thinking about them. One small way of doing this is by keeping a daily *positive journal*.

A positive daily journal is simply a brief journal where you highlight a few positive—and only positive—interactions that you have had that day. It is best to have it by the bedside and to jot down a few examples of positive interactions every night for as long as one year. It may seem like a lot of work to keep a positive journal but like the freight train initially starting its journey, it will need more fuel to start than when it reaches cruising speeds. The daily journal is the same. It may seem difficult to do and even to think of positive interactions but as you program your mind to more effectively see the positive interactions in a day, the daily journaling becomes far easier.

Keeping a daily positive journal is a small way to help recognize the progress you will make in your journey towards your true self and a more fulfilled life. There are many other things that you can do such as finding a support group, enlisting the aid of a friend, and even having a therapist help you along the way. Whatever path you choose for change, recognizing change and breaking it into stages helps to better illustrate your progress and helps you to maintain motivation until you find permanent change.

We will devote the next chapter to how to maintain motivation, as it is often the biggest barrier to lasting change. For now, take a look at the following exercises to help you through the various stages of change and growth.

EXERCISE FOR CHANGE:

Take time to write out or think about conceptualizing the three phases of change. Begin by looking at your life and family history. In the identification phase below, write out how your life may have created a false identity and write out your true identity. In part two, the understanding and correcting phase, write out how your false identity is being sustained in conversation, daily social interactions, and in internalized thoughts and dialogue. Write out specific goals you have to offset your struggles. Think about a clear definition and example of the final outcome. In part three, the maintenance phase, write out the positive daily interactions and the goals that you have accomplished for that day. Visualize having achieved your true identity. Write out a detailed description of your day and daily interactions as if you have already achieved the growth you are striving toward. Write out a detailed summary of your daily interaction as if you have already achieved the change and are now your true self. What would your behaviors look like now? How about the behaviors of others?

Beginning Phases for Change & Growth

1. **Identification Phase:**
   - *Looking back at my life, I understand my struggle to be:*

   _____

   _____

   _____

2. **Understanding and correcting phase:**
   - *Looking at my daily life and interactions, my struggle is evidenced by:*

   _____

   _____

   _____

   - *How I can correct these interactions is by:*

   _____

   _____

   _____

   - *When I have achieved change in my life and become who I am, it will look like:*

   _____

   _____

BECOME WHO YOU ARE

_____
_____
_____
_____
_____
_____
_____
_____
_____
_____

3. Maintenance Phase:
- **Positive daily Journal**
  Today what was positive was:

_____
_____
_____
_____
_____
_____

- **I noticed progress towards goals today in:**

_____

_____

_____

_____

_____

_____

Note: Remember to keep a daily positive journal where you highlight only positive events, comments, or interactions you have had, witnessed, or received to assist with recognizing your forward progress. It is a good idea to keep a positive journal for around 60 to 90 days minimum but, for best results, one year is recommended.

Chapter Eight

Maintaining Motivation For Change

*"Motivation is what gets you started.
Habit is what keeps you going."*

-Jim Ryun-

Once change has begun, the challenge then becomes to maintain the behaviors and your motivation until the changes you have made become habit and permanent. Although we touched on motivation in Chapter Seven, it is crucial to give this more thought to ensure that change and growth continues and can be sustained long enough to reduce the impact of the false self on the direction of your life.

Having the proper motivation is absolutely necessary if change is to occur and last over time. However, motivation is as independent and unique to each of us as a fingerprint. What motivates you for change is not necessarily the same as what motivates your friends, family, or others. It is important to find the motivation that works best for you so that the behaviors and changes for which you are striving can be sustained over a longer period of time. Without motivation or the emotional energy necessary for change, people fall back into old habits and never actualize change.

Finding the correct motivation is not as easy as it sounds. Often people utilize shortsighted emotional energy that stems from emotional reactions or aversion to situations like fear or punishment. Emotional motivation such as fear or punishment may be effective for immediate and short-term changes, but it is seldom effective in the long run. You need motivation that can last for the duration of the process and endure when the false self tries to combat growth with self-doubt and other obstacles.

Sustainable motivation comes not from negative emotions that can actually fuel the false self, but from positive emotions that fuel the true self. Negative emotional states such as fear or anger can be effective to start changes initially, but they do not last because the reactions to fear and negative emotional motivators will fade over time. For example, if your doctor tells you that you have high cholesterol and you may have a heart attack, you get motivated to change eating habits and start an exercise program. However, if after a few months, you start feeling better and have lower cholesterol rates, you may notice a loss in motivation for sustaining the abstemious behaviors and exercise program. Over time, you start to forget about the fear and once the fear aspect has worn off, often time people fall right back into the unhealthy eating habits that have led them to have high cholesterol in the first place. Fear and negative emotional states typically do not last long for motivation. Positive reward behavior can be more effective in maintaining performance and satisfaction than fear or punishment alone (Podsakoff, Todor, Grover, and Huber; 1984).

POSITIVE AND NEGATIVE MOTIVATION; WHY POSITIVE IS BETTER.

We often use negative images and thoughts for motivation, like being criticized by others, to move us forward when we are trying to change our behaviors. Although we are taught the punishment-avoidance philosophy for motivation in almost every aspect of our lives, many prominent psychologists including BF Skinner have found that punishment itself is never an effective reinforcement for permanent change. We learn to fear things for motivation such as "do it or else you will get fired," "you better not speed or you will get a ticket," or "do your homework or you will fail." In the short term, punishment can be used for changing behaviors, but it is not sustainable for the most part because punishment is often met with resentment, frustration, and rebellion.

To give you an example, imagine if your boss repeatedly threatened you that you would lose your job if you did not perform adequately. How would you feel with that constant threat and negative feedback hanging over your head each day for months? If every day, you were threatened to have your job taken from you, after a while you would begin to tire of the threats and say, "Just do it then! I don't care anymore!" The same holds true when you conjure up punitive images to try to motivate yourself to change your behavior based on this avoidance of punishment. Eventually, you call your own bluff and the motivation fades because the fear no longer is effective in maintaining the motivation for changing your behavior.

Now, let's say that you went to work and every day your boss stated that you had done a good job and have been working hard. Your boss further tells you that you and your efforts are greatly appreciated and he/she discusses the probability that a promotion will come in the end. Rather than using threats, when a person—in this case your boss—rewards your behavior and offers a promotion or other positive goal, you will most likely find that you feel more productive at work, are more enthusiastic about working longer hours, and generally feel more content with your life. You will be more likely to be productive and motivated to perform to the best of your abilities when your efforts are recognized and rewarded with positive praise or acknowledgement rather than when motivated by fear or intimidation.

By focusing on things that you *do* want rather than on what you *don't* want to happen, you can effectively sustain motivation and maintain a more optimistic mood overall than with fear alone. Living in fear and negativity often fuels the false self and causes you to more readily see the negativity in life and less opportunity for growth and happiness. Fear and avoidance can be powerful motivators but they can misdirect your energy and focus into looking backwards rather than forwards.

Setting positive goals allows for more self-expression, more independence, and allows you to feel that you have freely chosen your goals without having them forced upon you by others. Although we all need some form of emotional motivation to help fuel and motivate ourselves, positive motivations offer better motivation than no motivation at all or negative emotional motivators like fear or punishment. Viktor Frankl acknowledged this when he stated, "What man actually needs is not a tensionless state but rather the striving and struggling for a worthwhile goal, a freely chosen task" (127). By having a worthwhile long-term positive goal, we allow ourselves to have more sustained positive emotional energy that we can use to help with sustaining motivation for a longer period of time.

To capture and hold on to motivation and live a more fulfilled life, you will want to create a vivid positive visual outcome or goal for your efforts and reinforce that image daily. You will want to set daily small goals that can be accomplished readily but be able to hold onto a larger goal for the future. We have touched on this concept in earlier chapters but we will highlight it and provide more in-depth information here.

Using the exercise example once again, think of the final outcome of your results of all the time spent in the gym. Visualize a *realistic* goal for your efforts. Adopting unrealistic goals like losing fifty pounds in one month will only perpetuate the sense of failure and rapidly decrease motivation if the bar is set too high and you are unable to accomplish it. Knowing what a realistic long-term goal is for you will be paramount to your success so make sure that the change you want to see is set realistically for your life and abilities. Setting a realistic goal like losing fifty pounds in six months is better and more realistic than in a single month.

Once you have a realistic goal set for the future, you want to think of setting interim smaller realistic goals as well to maintain motivation until your goal is accomplished. If you have only one goal and the goal is set too far off, it will have less motivational reward than having short-term goals that lead to a larger final goal.

Let's get back to the example and say that your ultimate goal is to lose fifty pounds. Now that you have the goal, you will have to create a mental picture and imagine what the final goal visually looks like for you—a static picture of what you would visually look like if you lose the desired weight. Say, for example, how you would look on a beach in the Bahamas with your spouse. Whatever the final goal is for you, create it as clear as if you were looking at a photograph.

When you are setting your long-term goal, imagine what you would think, feel, and how people would realistically respond to you if your goal were accomplished. Devise a clear image in your mind of the final goal and precisely how you would feel and look when that goal was accomplished. After the picture of your final goal is concrete, vivid, and accurate, then you will want to set more manageable goals for the short run. Basically, each day, set smaller goals like working out for one hour, eating smaller meals, etc. that helps you to get closer to your ultimate goal.

Once you have long term goals and short term goals, then all you have to do is to give yourself positive accolades for getting through each day's goal. While you are working out for that hour, imagine that picture of your final goal while saying and noticing only positive traits of yourself or that people have said to you that you later put into a positive daily journal. If you notice yourself saying negative comments at any time during your workout or the day, change them immediately to avoid the resurgence of the false self and the waning of your motivation.

Whether it is working out, changing destructive behaviors, or managing emotional states such as depression or anxiety, the same concept still applies. Set small daily goals, monitor any and all positive aspects in a daily journal, and have a realistic final goal with detailed images. Your motivation to stay the course of change will be more readily sustained. Always remember that what changes behavior more permanently is positive reinforcement, not punishment.

Most motivation tends to be stifled because people can more often see problems or obstacles to beginning or maintaining behaviors rather than the positive outcomes. They don't go to the gym because they think of the parking hassles or the pain they will experience the following day.

They do not leave the house because they think of all the difficult social situations they will encounter. Whatever it is, people often call into reality a negative picture of the future and it paralyzes them from moving forward and destroys the motivation for change.

This negative thinking can rob a person of seeing the growth they have made and derails long-term motivation. To experience continued growth and to maintain long-term motivation, changing the way you think and interpret situations is a must. Sometimes, success is right in front of us but we are blinded by our negative thinking or interpretation of our situation or expectations based on our past experiences and beliefs. We may see a situation as an example of failure when in actuality we have shown progress. By changing the way you think and perceive situations, you will begin to see many situations and areas of growth that you never realized before and continue with motivation for much longer than without changing your perception.

NO SUCH THING AS FAILURE

When it comes to motivation, how you interpret situations and setbacks are paramount. When we are examining our progress, there is no such thing as failure if you can take an objective look at your situation. We frequently see failure in situations where progress has actually been made. To give you an example of this concept:

Joey was an aspiring marathon runner. He had never run a serious marathon against opponents before. He signed up for a 20K run and placed three hundred out of one thousand runners. He lamented his placement swearing to give up his desire to run another marathon. He said, "I did awful. I placed 300th!" I looked at him and said, "Yeah, you ranked among the top one-third of professional runners. That sounds pretty awful for your first run." He looked at me for a moment and smiled. "I guess I did. It doesn't sound that bad when you say it like that."

As in the case of Joey, we often measure our failures rather than our accomplishments. Joey placed in the top one-third of trained professional runners on his first run, which is impressive. However, he opted to look at how many others placed ahead of him rather than how many professional runners in front of he had placed. By looking at objective data for your accomplishments, you can more accurately see your success and progress.

As with any path, there are steps that need to be accomplished. Not all goals will be accomplished with one fell swoop. By keeping a realistic concept of your accomplishment and looking for success rather than failure, you rob failure of its debilitating effects, even if you did not accomplish your goal. Failure is not failure. Failure is the record to break on your next attempt. Failure is an internal concept and is an inaccurate interpretation of your actions and performance. In reality, you have only benchmarks, not failure. The most successful people in life do not see failure; they see opportunity and lack of success as a learning tool.

Almost everything as far as success goes is a matter of subjective interpretation. Those that we see as optimists attribute failure as a single problem resulting from temporary circumstances, whereas pessimists attribute failure as inherent traits and as personal (Seligman, 2002). For example, an optimist may say something like, "That was a bummer that I missed out on the promotion. I really wanted that. The timing must not have been right. I will get it on the next time around." A pessimist would say something like, "I can't believe I missed out on the promotion. I am a failure, and they must hate me to overlook me. I will never get that promotion!"

When we set out to accomplish something and we fall short of that goal, we berate ourselves and say, "I can't believe I failed! Why bother?" By not seeing the success in our attempt, we short circuit our motivation and overlook our progress. Change does not typically go without incident. There are obstacles, setbacks, and challenges to any form of emotional growth. It is these challenges that make the reward of change so sweet.

My point here with not seeing failure in our attempts is not to be disgustingly optimistic; rather it is to highlight that too many of us look for failure in our success rather than the success in our progress. We are human and there are always some rewards for being negative. We have all complained about a product or service and received something free or had our problem remedied expeditiously when we were mad. We are aware of reinforcement for being negative. However, there are benefits for focusing on the positive that may not be so readily apparent but are far more effective and healthier for you and your life.

If you spend a day consciously and deliberately searching out positive events and situations, you would marvel at what you will find. Accomplishment abounds in your life. When you look for failure, no matter how many times you succeed, you will always see failure. When you look for positive, it will overshadow perceived failure and eventually failure will become nonexistent. Take away failure and you take away anxiety, depression, and low self-esteem, and add success, motivation, and confidence.

Teaching yourself to see the success and growth rather than failure in situations will take time and practice. However, retraining yourself to see positive in your tasks is relatively simple. The positive daily journal is the first step in retraining you. Reframing is when you simply try to spin a situation to where you see it as a positive only. For example, you get a speeding ticket. You can think of all the negative situations like insurance costs increasing, the hassle of traffic court, etc. You can reframe this by stating to yourself, "That is a bummer to have to pay but I was speeding and it is a wake-up call for me to slow down and focus on my driving so no one gets hurt in the future." You can reframe any situation with practice. Practice daily if there is a situation that bothers you or you see as negative.

Motivation over time is easy to maintain with the proper short and long term goals. It helps to be able to understand and be patient with setbacks and reframe them when they occur. If you can see the positive and the growth during your journey, lasting change and a better positive mood is bound to occur. Take a look at the exercise below to help you with your goals and motivation until change becomes permanent.

POSITIVE FINAL GOAL:

Write out a clear picture of the change you want to see with as much detail as you can.

_____

_____

_____

POSITIVE DAILY GOALS:

List short-term daily goals that you can readily accomplish and that will lead you toward your final larger goal.

_____

_____

_____

EXERCISE FOR RECOGNIZING STRENGTHS:

List five of your strengths and a phrase or sentence that supports it. Whenever you receive negative feedback or begin to have negative emotions or declining motivation, say five of your strengths to remind yourself that setbacks do not define you.

- **Strength 1:**_____

  _____

  *Supporting phrase:*_____

  _____

- **Strength 2:**_____

  _____

  *Supporting phrase:*_____

  _____

- **Strength 3:**_____

  _____

  *Supporting phrase:*_____

  _____

- **Strength 4:**_____

  _____

  *Supporting phrase:*_____

  _____

- **Strength 5:**_____

  _____

*Supporting phrase:*_____

_____

REFRAMING EXERCISE FOR MAINTAINING MOTIVATION AND OVERCOMING OBSTACLES:

Take some time to list the five areas of growth that you may not have initially have seen for yourself. Even if the growth is small, write it out so that you can see the positive momentum in your life.

The areas I have seen growth are:

1. _____
2. _____
3. _____
4. _____
5. _____

The negative situation that happened was:
Write out situations that you perceived as negative or aversive.

1. _____
2. _____
3. _____
4. _____
5. _____

How I can reframe this negative situation to positive is:
Now write out the positive spin on the negative situations described above using only the positive interpretation or outcome.

1._____

2._____

3._____

4._____

5._____

Chapter Nine

Improving And Maintaining Your Mood

"Happiness is when what you think, what you say, and what you do are in harmony."

-Mahatma Gandhi-

Moods are an essential element of the human experience. Moods are responsible for creative expressions and our displays of love, anger, and joy. We experience emotions to some degree daily and in almost every human interaction. Moods can range from despair to jubilation and everywhere in between. Moods that are positive such as happiness, contentment, and joy can help you to more fully express yourself, live a more fulfilled life, and can allow you to achieve stronger and more fulfilling interpersonal interactions. Low moods such as depression or sadness are likely to cause people to have more physical complaints of pain, have a shorter life span and report a diminished quality of life overall (Seligman, 2002).

Even though some low moods like depression can be a good sign indicating your potential for growth, low moods are not something that we want to remain in for long. Remaining in a depressed state can limit your energy and positive outlook that is necessary for change and for you to live a more fulfilled life. However, maintaining a positive mood has become increasingly more difficult with the rapid evolution of today's society and the changing demands of family, work, and social networks.

Modern society has adapted and changed to a growing population faster than our biology has been allowed to adapt to the changes. Our bodies were designed for humans to roam out in the open savannah amid fresh air, sun, and to be physically active. Now, within the last one hundred years or so, we have radically shifted the physical and environmental demands for which our bodies were programmed. We have become sedentary, enduring constant stress from multiple sources, and remain locked in sunless office spaces during the day while we rapidly consume a high fat and poor nutritional diet. Our bodies have drastically shifted environments and the shift has caused many of us to experience various low moods and even depression due to the limitation of sunlight, physical exercise, and poor nutrition diets.

To have and maintain a positive mood, you need to be aware of both internal and external contributors that include personal and environmental factors that can influence your mood. Things such as diet, light, movement, perception, social interaction, self-expression, and laughter can all impact your mood to some degree. In the following sections, we will tackle each of these areas and discuss ways that you can improve the areas that may be contributing to the low mood.

DIET AND MOOD

Food plays an important role in your energy level, your overall health, and how you feel. The food you choose to consume influences the neurotransmitters—the chemicals in your brain that contribute to "feeling good." The neurotransmitter called *serotonin* has been shown to affect mood and self-esteem. Too little of this neurotransmitter and you experience low self-esteem, low energy, and low mood or depression. Diets that are poor or are too low in calories and/or skipped meals can reduce your serotonin levels (Ross 2002).

Diets have become a stronger contributor for our mood because our diets have become more processed and are more nutritionally deficient than ever before. Out of convenience and time constraints, many of us have resorted to highly processed "fast foods" or foods that are convenient but that are nutritionally poor and insufficient to meet your necessary dietary and nutritional requirements. By increasing your intake of less refined foods that are high in protein such as turkey, beef, pork, dairy products, chicken, venison, and eggs, it may help your body to produce serotonin and help to improve your mood (Somer 1995).

To keep up with our busy and fast-paced lifestyle, many of us have turned to various stimulants such as coffee or energy drinks. Stimulants such as caffeine not only interfere with sleep but also can interfere with the production of serotonin. In addition, Aspartame, the artificial sweetener found in most "sugar free" food items, has ingredients that can act much like a stimulant and interfere with serotonin production (Ross 2002).

Serotonin levels not only can affect our moods but the way we feel and can manifest in physical symptoms. Here are some signs that Ross (2002) has listed that may indicate low serotonin levels:

- Gut and heart problems
- Sleep problems
- Fibromyalgia and other pain conditions
- Cravings for carbohydrates, alcohol and certain drugs.

It is not only what you eat that can influence your mood, it is also when and how much you eat that can influence mood. Research has shown that those that disperse meals evenly throughout the day maintain a more even temperament and are less prone to fatigue, and depression (Somer p.275).

You have heard that breakfast is the most important meal. Well, research has backed that claim. People that skip breakfast have a more difficult time managing their weight and have lower levels of energy later in the day (Somer 1995). Starting your day with a good breakfast, improving your diet with foods rich in nutrients that can increase serotonin production and avoiding stimulants can help improve your overall mood and help you to maintain a positive and consistent mood. Meeting with a nutritionist or nutritional counselor may help you to set up a proper diet to maximize serotonin production and help towards improving your mood and overall health.

LIGHT AND MOOD

It takes more than diet to help improve mood. Sunlight is crucial to maintaining our mood. Sunlight is also a necessary element for improving serotonin production and helping to maintain a positive mood. Our bodies are designed for more sunlight and physical exercise then we currently receive. Vitamin D is an essential element for maintaining mood, especially in older adults, and sunlight helps with vitamin D production (Stewart & Hirani; 2010). Until recently, only sunlight could produce vitamin D, as there were no readily available nutritional supplements for vitamin D replacement. Now, vitamin D supplementation is recommended commonly to increase vitamin D levels. Lack of vitamin D has been linked to low mood, decreased energy, and more recently also to medical conditions such as fibromyalgia (Al-Dabbagh TQ 2012).

Our bodies were designed for more sunlight than we currently receive. Our modern society and work environments have reduced our exposures to natural light by having us indoor more often during times when the sunlight is most intense. We need sunlight to help with production of vitamin D and with serotonin production. By getting at least fifteen minutes of sunlight exposure, you can drastically increase your vitamin D production rate and increase serotonin production that is essential for mood and self-esteem.

Sunlight helps with serotonin production because there is a part of the brain connected to the optic nerve that helps to produce serotonin when light is received in the eye above roughly 800 lumens. When there is increased light, such as found in the summer and spring months, your brain will produce more serotonin than in the darker months of winter and fall. Have you noticed that in summer you have more energy than you do in winter? Sunlight affects mood. Many people get what is known as SAD (Seasonal Affective Disorder) where limited sunlight exposure creates mild depression in fall and winter months due in large part to diminished serotonin production with decreased light exposure.

Light can impact mood. Energy levels are due in large part to past survival mechanisms. The cold, cloudy days represent more dangers from the natural world than would sunny days that typically bring more hospitable weather. The body regulates energy levels in darker months because if you have tons of energy to roam the hillside in winter, you might get stuck in a snowstorm and freeze to death. By reducing serotonin production in winter months, it slows you down and limits you from leaving the safety of shelter. When the seasons warm, the light is more intense and the days longer, and it is typically safer for you to roam around than it would be with the worry of being stuck in a snowstorm.

Although our link to sunlight and energy was designed for survival mechanisms, this survival mechanism is now a detriment given our declining exposure to sunlight year round. Our modern society and decreased sunlight exposure has effectively caused a perpetual winter and leaves our energy and mood more sub-optimal than if we received more light exposure. Hence getting more sunlight exposure, ideally at least getting light exposure for longer than 15 minutes per day, can help with increasing your serotonin production, energy levels, and overall vitamin D levels.

MOVEMENT AND MOOD

Movement and exercise are some of the quickest ways to improve your mood and increase serotonin production. A part of the motor cortex in your brain stimulates serotonin production when you move repeatedly. Have you noticed that when you are anxious you chew your nails, tap your fingers, or shake your leg? With increased serotonin, anxiety is lessened. During times of stress, your toe tapping, nail biting, leg shaking is actually helping you to manage your stress chemically by causing your brain to release more serotonin. Repetitive movements such as toe tapping, leg shaking, drumming your fingers on a desk, all act to produce serotonin.

Running, working out, playing football or any other form of physical activity does relatively the same thing to a greater degree. Moving large muscles releases endogenous opioids and other neurotransmitters such as serotonin. The results on mood and self-esteem are noticeable if you recall how you felt the last time you went to work out or jog. You may have noticed that you felt better, less stressed, that problems seem less severe after you have jogged, worked out, hiked, or exercised. Now you know why.

The larger the muscles you stimulate during exercise and movement, the more serotonin you are likely to produce. Setting up some form of daily exercise, including as little as 30 minutes of walking three times a week, is incredibly helpful for maintaining a positive mood. Exercise improves your mood and when your mood is beginning to improve, you are better able to recall the happy times and think of a more positive future. If you combine exercise with sunlight, you increase serotonin production even further. If you can exercise outdoors, do so. Just use sun block and take appropriate precautions from overexposure to sun.

PERCEPTION AND MOOD

There are more than just physical and environmental contributors to mood. How we interpret situations can impact our moods and our moods themselves can impact our interpretation of situations. For example, when you are depressed, you may be able to pick out depressed faces in a crowd easier and will attend to negative feedback from the environment faster than if you are in a positive mood. Once your mind is focused on a mood like depression, your brain subconsciously seeks out environmental evidence of the mood.

To give you an example, let's say that you may be interested in buying a green Toyota Camry. Once you think about the green Toyota, your mind will begin to subconsciously attend to and seek out that information in the environment. You may be driving down the freeway talking to your passenger and notice that your head turns and your eyes have shifted to a passing green Toyota. All of a sudden, you may be amazed at how many green Toyota Camrys you are now noticing during the day. Your mind began to subconsciously process information and select out all of the passing cars, calling your attention to the information (i.e. green Toyota Camry) that you have been interested in and thinking about.

The same concept applies to when you are depressed. When you are depressed, the false identity is subconsciously looking for things in the environment that are reinforcing to the negative data or the negative self-perception. Without a positive mood to offset the negative filter, your mind is apt to see events and situations in a more negative light. Additionally, when your mood is low, your mind is likely to accept more criticism from people and to have more negative interactions overall because your subconscious mind is looking for situations to reinforce these negative moods and self-perceptions.

When your mood is low or you are under emotional stressors such as anxiety and/or depression, it will limit your ability to have free and unhindered expression of your true self and accurate perceptions of neutral situations. Depression and other negative mood states will limit your ability to see the positive interactions throughout your day due to the filter that is subconsciously operating. Low moods can prohibit you from expressing your true self due to the emotional interference and the resulting stimuli.

Our memory, our ability for decision-making, and our ability to objectively look at positive future outcomes are all impaired during times of stress or depression when your mind is impacted by negative moods. When you are in a depressed or altered state, you brain more readily recalls memories that coincide with that negative emotional or cognitive state. This is due to what researchers identified in 1937 as *state dependent learning*. (Girden, Culter).

State dependent learning ties memories and perceptions to various emotional or chemically modified states. Memories are stored bio-chemically.

The stronger the emotion during the formation of a memory or of an event, the stronger the memory will become. To give you an example: Have you ever noticed how when you are angry with your partner and you begin to have an argument how much quicker and with precise clarity that you can recall all the things in the past that have angered you? Before the argument, you likely thought little of past injustices or hurt. However, what now started out as a minor irritant turned into you recounting an entire list of things that have angered you in the past with astonishing clarity. This flood of angry memories of past arguments and past hurt only happens because of state dependent learning. When you are calm, you do not have access to those memories. When you become angry, the neuropathways that created those past memories are triggered and allow you to better access those memories.

Perception and mood go hand in hand. When depressed, you can better recall all the memories and things that have reinforced the depression with greater ease. You are likely to interpret neutral information in a more negative light because the memories or events you experienced when in a low mood previously are more easily recalled when you are in a similar negative state. You can more easily remember all the negative self-talk, times of rejection, humiliation, and any other situations that occurred when you are in a low mood than when you are experiencing a happy mood. When you are depressed, it may feel as though you have always been depressed and that the depression and unhappiness may feel as though they are permanent and unending. The good thing is that the reverse applies as well. When you are in a good mood, state dependent learning says that you are more likely to easily recall memories where you were in a good mood. Keeping your spirits up, looking at the positive, and training your mind to interpret neutral information in more positive light can help to improve your mood. By maintaining a positive outlook and a positive mood, you will be better able to focus on your true self and achieve the final outcome of change quicker and with greater sustainability.

There are various things in daily life that you can do to improve your mood, to shift your perception to more a positive focus, and to keep the false identity from hindering the attainment of a sustained positive mood. The most important and crucial step to this end is to continue with the positive daily journaling. Positive daily journaling is crucial in order to minimize the impact of negative perceptions by retraining your brain to actively seek out positive situations and interactions. By actively learning to train your brain to see the positive in situations, you then improve your state dependent learning to filter out negative self-views and to improve your outlook for neutral or potentially negative situations. When you are able to maintain a consistent positive mood, you are better able to interact with others, pay closer attention to small signs of growth with greater ease, and are better able to recall the events of the day with a more accurate viewpoint.

SOCIAL INTERACTIONS AND MOOD

Social interactions are an important element for helping you to sustain a positive mood because much of our self-appraisal is due to social feedback. Having authentic and healthy social interactions is crucial to having a healthy self-concept and a positive mood. If social interactions continue to go awry, we tend to become self-critical and unhappy overall.

By nature, humans were designed to have social interactions. We need and desire some form of social connection. However, many of us either continue with unhealthy social interactions based on our past experiences or engage in new ones based on an inauthentic self from a false identity that can impair our social interactions. Maintaining social and interpersonal interactions based on your true identity or an authentic self will improve the quality of your social interactions, add an increased sense of fulfillment to social interactions, and allow for overall increased positive feedback from others.

Being authentic in social interactions can be difficult because each social group comes with different expectations, different rules, and different interests that bind them together. When false identities are lingering within, we tend to sacrifice more of our true self and try to act in a way in which we will be most readily accepted by others or in ways in which we are most familiar with our past interpersonal interaction. This sacrifice comes at a cost. Continuously changing and adapting to groups or social situations makes it more difficult for you to see your true self because you are trying to be accepted rather than being yourself and allowing healthy social connections to develop. By denying access to your own identity, your own wishes, and your own dreams, you ultimately sacrifice the authentic social feedback and connection that provides a sense of fulfillment.

As soon as we deviate from our authentic/true self in social situations or interactions, we open ourselves up to negative thoughts and negative self-talk. In social interactions, when you act differently from what you feel inside or act in a way that is contrary to what you believe, it typically causes a form of internalized distress that researchers like Leon Festinger (1957) have called *cognitive dissonance*. This cognitive dissonance can be the emotional experience of your conscience. It is the mild distress you experience when acting contrary to your conscience or what you believe to be your internalized self-representation.

For example, if you hold a certain belief such as "I am honest" and you tell a lie, even a white lie, you will exhibit a certain form of distress or discomfort that can manifest in physical and mental symptoms. The emotional and physical responses that you feel when you are in cognitive dissonance is what lie detectors utilize to register if you are lying or not. With some cognitive dissonance, the physical reactions can be increases in perspiration, respiration, and heart rate. Think back to how it felt when you last told someone a white lie. Did you think about it after you told the lie? How did it feel? Did your heart rate increase? Did you lose sleep over it thinking about the lie and the consequences of someone finding out?

The more you experience cognitive dissonance in social settings, the greater the anxiety and the fear for engaging in social situations. Social interactions are important for emotional health and longevity. Depriving yourself of positive social interaction increases opportunities for depression and isolation. Engaging in social interaction in an authentic way allows you to be more proactive rather than reactive in social settings and with social and interpersonal interactions.

To have authentic social interactions, you first have to know your strengths and be able to express yourself. Knowing your strengths and repeating them daily and prior to any social interaction can increase your self-esteem and confidence. You additionally should be aware of the false identity you have and know the behaviors that trigger your false self. Sometimes having good social interactions means knowing which people to avoid. If someone is overly domineering and you have a propensity to be submissive, you may want to avoid social interaction with that person so that you do not stifle your own needs and identity.

Knowing your strengths, seeking out healthy social interactions with people that share your interests and morals, and being able to express yourself freely can add overall quality in social interactions and help you maintain a positive mood.

SELF-EXPRESSION AND MOOD

Self-expression is an important aspect to happiness and growth. It consists of direct actions such as behaviors and communication but can also include indirect means such as creative and artistic outlets. Self-expression is not simply the ability to be outspoken. It is about maintaining a consistent connection to who you are and an unhindered expression of that self to others. Many people think that by saying something mean or derogatory that they are simply expressing themselves. This may be a form of self-expression, but hurtful and destructive communication should be used with caution. It is typically a sign that effective communication has broken down and rather than the person expressing himself or herself, the person is trying to hurt, lash out, and otherwise be offensive.

True self-expression involves identifying and responding to the true emotion within and not just the surface reaction to the initial emotion. For example, anger is almost always a reaction to another emotion. Anger often arises when you feel hurt, vulnerable, threatened, bullied, etc. Anger is a defensive emotional state rather than a form of self-expression. Many people choose to bypass the true emotion that they feel and jump right to the protective emotional state of anger. True self-expression involves a thoughtful moment of introspection before responding. Anger is a reactionary emotion and often involves hurtful behavior and lashing out.

Let's say your friend Jenny says something hurtful about your appearance. Jenny says, *"That dress makes you look fat!"* A natural response may be to retaliate with anger and then make a snide or angry comment back. True self-expression would be to say something like, *"Wow, Jenny, I feel really hurt by that statement."* By choosing to say how Jenny's comment hurt you, you free up the space for your true self to find expression and allow for real communication to occur rather than the escalation of anger. If you were to show Jenny aggression and anger right back, communication would escalate and often result in an argument. By making the comment to Jenny that you were hurt, it reduces the friction and increases the likelihood that Jenny would respond with less anger and likely be apologetic or sympathetic.

People often hide their emotions and limit self-expression due to fear of being vulnerable. Many people fear that if they show emotions or vulnerability that others will receive them poorly. How often have you stood by while a friend was treated poorly by someone and when you asked why they did not stand up for themselves, you were told something like, *"I did not want to make them mad."*

The fear of being rejected by others prevents many people from speaking their mind, speaking from the heart, and ultimately keeps them locked within their own isolated world. However, by expressing yourself, you often allow the person to see your true self and ultimately end up having more meaningful and deeper connections than not expressing yourself.

Self-expression can include creative and artistic endeavors like writing, painting, or singing that allow you to put something into the world. Creativity can be expressed in many forms such as painting, sculpting, writing, singing, or making music. Music is a powerful motivational force for maintaining health and increasing vitality. A study done by Midori Koga (2001) found that immersion in musical experiences through listening, singing and movement activities resulted in lower levels of anxiety and depression. It also led to an increase by as much as 90% in levels of Human Growth Hormone, which helps to increase energy and sexual function, while causing fewer wrinkles and cases of osteoporosis.

The more that you share and allow the true self-expression of your emotions, especially the positive ones, the greater the positive feedback you will receive. It is oftentimes more acceptable to complain than it is to express joy, but that will yield far less long-term gains. All emotions are infectious. Share joy, you receive joy. Express misery, you receive misery in return. For an experiment, try one day to be determined to bring a smile to the face of someone. If it is your significant other or family member, make sincere compliments on his or her appearance, attitude, or whatever it is that you appreciate about them or their actions. Look for any positive quality about that person that you respect and hold that in your mind. You will find that the more you give, the more you receive. You will find that the more you look for positive things about others, the more positive things you will see in yourself and the better your mood will become.

Self-expression and having creative outlets are important to maintaining mood. Practice saying or doing one thing each day that is a form of self-expression and you will notice a more positive mood, a lighter spirit, and an overall improved sense of wellbeing. Don't be afraid to compliment a friend, to tell someone close to you how you feel, and above all, don't be afraid to be creative, to laugh, and express joy with others.

LAUGHTER AND MOOD

It seems that as we get older, humor becomes a less important aspect in our lives and, as adults, we laugh much less than when we were children (Abramovitz, 2000). It is a shame that we lose the importance of humor as we get older because the reputed benefits of humor abound. The benefits include the alleviation of pain and increased quality of life in terminally ill patients, an increase in released endorphins and improvements in natural killer cell activity. Laughter is also an effective coping device to modulate stress and is an excellent device for expanding one's network of friends (Franzini, 2001).

Some researchers suggest that humor may help with our mental health and self-esteem because it helps to prevent negative self-pity and can help us feel more in control of our situation (Abramovitz, 2000). In addition, laughter influences your health by directly stimulating your immune system to ward off viruses and cancers. It can also increase the number of antibodies that fight infection, lowers stress hormones in the bloodstream, lowers blood pressure, and helps the cardiovascular system by expelling stale air and causing the heart to beat faster (Abramovitz, 2000). Humor and laughing are like exercising. Imagine exercising outdoors on a sun-filled day while laughing. How good would you feel? You may look funny but your mood would be great!

We have covered some of the areas that can contribute to helping you maintain a positive mood. Maintaining a positive mood is a combination of physical and psychological elements that all make up how you see yourself and the world. By changing basic things such as diet, how much you exercise, light exposure, monitoring your negative self-statements, and having creative outlets you can greatly improve your changes for sustaining a positive mood. Use the checklist below to help remind you of the basics for maintaining your positive mood.

CHECKLIST FOR MAINTAINING A POSITIVE MOOD

- **Exercise three times a week** ☐
- **Sunlight Exposure** ☐
- **Self-Expression** ☐
- **Balanced Diet** ☐
- **Humor/Laugh** ☐
- **Creative Outlet** ☐

Chapter Ten

Putting It All Into Daily Practice

"Knowledge is of no value unless you put it into practice."

-Anton Chekhov-

Now that you have read all the chapters in the book, understand your struggle, how to improve yourself, improve your moods, know how to maintain motivation, how to improve your communications, and improve your relationships, it is time to put it all into daily application. Since, up to this point in your life, you have established and maintained a daily routine template based on the false identity, it is time to implement a new one based on your true self. It is time to have your true self emerge, to change the daily routine template to match your true identity, and to put all that you have learned into daily practice. You change one step at a time, which means taking everything one day at a time with realistic and manageable doses.

Begin each day with the mental photograph described in chapters seven and eight and the practice of reminding yourself of the positive aspects of yourself and your strengths. Begin each day with the exercise of programming your mind with positive self-traits through positive daily journaling and you will be better able to see positive interactions throughout the day. With a clear picture of the end result in mind, you move the positive self-image into the present and project that image onto others. If you begin the day with a negative attitude, you inadvertently look for all that reinforces that view in yourself and in others. Begin with positives and you set up positive interactions throughout the day and your mind searches out positive situations and outcomes automatically.

Throughout the day, monitor what you say and the situations that may be challenging or are reinforcing the false self. Knowing that you may have a predisposition to subconsciously implant messages in others will help you modify your communication. In the morning, as you mention the positive traits and strengths, think of one overall message that you want to send to someone. For example, say to yourself, "*I am confident and successful.*" Repeating this general mantra throughout the day before any interaction and being mindful of this statement when you are communicating will help implement a positive meta-message throughout your conversation.

With each interaction with significant others, be sure to provide positive feedback and statements. State clearly what you want throughout the day and comment on the positive behaviors of your significant other.

End the day by listing all the positive interactions you have experienced in a basic journal or simply spend a few moments thinking of only the positive interactions. Omit negative interactions and self-statements. If you notice any creeping in, change them immediately. Reframe any negative situation that comes to mind and find the positive interaction no matter how insignificant. Allow only positive statements and thoughts to filter through your mind in the evening and throughout the day to reprogram and establish new neuropathways to develop that reinforce and strengthen your true identity.

Repetition builds and reinforces neuropathways. The more you think something, the easier it is to see it and believe it. Use the daily checklist to provide structure and remind you of the behaviors you need to engage in for the day and the strengths that you possess.

Practice these basic steps described in the preceding chapters and those highlighted on the checklist below each day and maintaining growth will become habitual like riding a bicycle. You will begin to perform positive interactions and think positive thoughts without conscious thought. Even if it feels a bit awkward at first, continue on. With repetition comes belief because you will begin to see how when you modify your internal world, the external world will follow. If you don't believe it to be true, no one else will. You have to believe in yourself, believe in your strengths, and believe in the process of change. Think positive self-images, make positive self-statements, teach others how to meet your needs and make positive statements to you, and then you will have the combination necessary to rebuild your life and become who you are and who you were meant to be.

Daily checklist
- Began morning with positive statements ☐
- Visualize mental photograph of true self ☐
- Recognize Strengths throughout the day ☐
- Reinforce positive meta-message ☐
- Reinforced positive behaviors of others ☐
- Put my needs out clearly for my partner ☐
- Daily Positive Journaling ☐
- End the day with positive self-reflection ☐

References

Abramovitz, M. (2000). Humor can heal. *Current Health 2*; Highland Park. 27 (4) pp25-27.

Festinger, L. (1957). *A Theory of Cognitive Dissonance.* Stanford, CA: Stanford University Press.

Frankl, V (1984). Man's Search for Meaning. Pocket Books. New York

J. Douglas Bremner, M.D.; Meena Narayan, M.D.; Eric R. Anderson; Lawrence H. Staib, Ph.D.; Helen L. Miller, M.D.; Dennis S. Charney, M.D.; *Hippocampal Volume Reduction in Major Depression. Am J Psychiatry 2000;157:115-118.*

Franzini, L.R. (2001) Humor in therapy: The case for training therapists in its uses and risks. *The Journal of General Psychology*; Provincetown, 128 (2) pgs0-193

Girden, E., Culler, E., (1937) *Journal of Comparative Psychology, 23(2),* 261–274.

Koga, M. (2001). The music making and wellness project *The American Music Teacher*; Cincinnati; 51 (2) p18-22.

McCann, J. C. Ames, B. N. Is there convincing biological or behavioral evidence linking vitamin D deficiency to brain dysfunction?. FASEB J. 2008 Apr; 22 (4): 982-1001.

Markman, M., Stanley, S., Blumburg, S., (2001). Fighting For Your Marriage. San Francisco. Jossey-Bass.

Nierenberg, Gerard I., Calero, Henry H. (1973) Meta-Talk: Hidden Meanings in Conversations. Cornerstone Library.

Podsakoff, P.M., Todor, W, D., Grover, R.A., and Huber, V. L., (1984). Situational moderators of leader reward and punishment behavior: Fact of fiction? *Organiizational Behavior and Human Performance*, 34, 21-63.

Preston, J. (2001) Lift your mood now: Simple things you can do to beat the blues. New Harbinger Publications. Oakland.

Rogers, C.R. (1959). A theory of therapy, personality and interpersonal relationships, as developed in the client-centered framework. In S. Koch (ed.). *Psychology: A study of science. (pp. 184-256)*. N.Y.: McGraw Hill.

Rogers, C.R (1961). *On becoming a person.* Boston: Houghton Mifflin.

Rogers, C.R (1965). A humanistic conception of man. In R.E. Farson (ed.) *Science and human affairs.* California: Science and Behavior Books Inc.

(1977). *Carl Rogers on personal power.* N.Y.: Delacorte Press.

Ross, J. (2002) The Mood Cure; The Four Step Program to Rebalance Your Emotional Chemistry and Rediscover Your Natural Sense of Well-being. Penguin Books. New York.

Seligmam, M (2002) Authentic Happiness; using the new positive psychology to realize your potential for lasting fulfillment. Free Press. New York.

Segal, Z., Williams, J. Gemar, M. (1996). Psychological Medicine, Vol 26 (2) http://uk.cambridge.org/journals/psm/ US: Cambridge University Press.

Somer, E. (1995). Food & Mood; The Complete Guide to Eating Well and Feeling Your Best. Henry Holt. New York.

Stewart, R. Hirani, V. Relationship between vitamin D levels and depressive symptoms in older residents from a national survey population. Psychosom Med. 2010 Sep; 72 (7): 608-12.

Al-Dabbagh TQ. The relation between vitamin D deficiency and fibromyalgia syndrome in women. Saudi Med J. 2011 Sep;32(9):925-9.

www.ingramcontent.com/pod-product-compliance
Lightning Source LLC
Chambersburg PA
CBHW061656040426
42446CB00010B/1761